APPRAISAL FEASIBILITY STUDY ETHICS BUSINESS VALUATION CONSULTANCY

APPRAISAL FEASIBILITY STUDY ETHICS BUSINESS VALUATION CONSULTANCY

DR. TOMASITO Z. ACADEMIA, ED. D

PARTRIDGE

To order additional copies of this book, contact
Toll Free 800 101 2657 (Singapore)
Toll Free 1 800 81 7340 (Malaysia)
orders.singapore@partridgepublishing.com

www.partridgepublishing.com/singapore

REALM REALTY
REAL ESTATE

APPRAISAL

FEASIBILITY STUDY

ETHICS

BUSINESS VALUATION

CONSULTANCY

Dr. Tomasito Z. Academia, Ed.D

PREFACE

LIGHT LIGHT

HEAVY HEAVY

RISK REWARD

This book begins with the basics of mathematics that is frequently encountered in the practice of real estate. As much as possible, its use is based on the trend and flow of the practice from the standpoint of a salesperson, broker, appraiser, valuer, consultant, environmental planner and as an educator.

Interest in real estate has increased faster in recent years upon the advent and transition from the Department of Trade and Industry (DTI), through the Bureau of Trade Regulatory Board and Industry (BTRCP), as mandated through its MO 39 and on to Professional Regulation Commission (PRC), onward to PRB-RES: from salesmanship, brokerage, appraisal, consultancy, public assessment, and to urban and regional planning.

Now the new realm and emerging real estate industry has come to full fruition.

This book becomes handy for banks, lenders, developers, students and professionals for the theory and practice of real estate. This **Real Estate Guidebook** comes into being, as an answer and clamor for a domestic and pure Pilipino blooded author as a contribution in whatever manner it may deem fit.

Most of the problems in the series of Time Value of Money concept and principles are being illustrated sequentially from cash flow diagram to the use of formula by the use of common calculator and double checked by Excel program of Microsoft. This way, tremendous pressure is put into the preparation of this book. It is worth the challenge! This book is designed for both academic and professional use. It is meant to provide a greater leeway in the use of different approaches to problems solving and come up with its prudent solutions.

This book prepares oneself to understand the risks and rewards associated in the different ways in the manner of investing and financing from the highest and best land use as state local government unit (LGU) zoned with its corresponding local passed ordinances as called for in its mandated city/municipality comprehensive land use plan **(CLUP).** Imply put, the applicability is for anyone who desires to upgrade himself in its uses as reference to his real estate practice needs.

Real estate investment in income-producing properties requires careful analysis of many variables and contingencies that project educated assumptions to come up with the expected profitability. The framework of investors concern and expectation is profitability. In as much as to its degree of specialization required,

This book is intended to touch on many topics, as much as possible. This is a series of subject processes from real estate brokerage, real estate appraisal, business valuation, project feasibility studies, basics of environmental impact assessment to urban economics.

The investment process forms the foundation for real estate investment analysis and strategy. There are good investment decisions arrived at and others were poorly executed, this study were also part of a strategy and business planning, through it all, it's always a good alternative to refer to or hire a real estate consultant.

This book is written, therefore, from this viewpoint and the needs of the student, real estate practitioners, engineers, consultants a sound understanding of the basic aspects of economics, finance, appraisal, valuation and real estate consultancy. Cash flow diagram, formula understanding and its derivation, calculator computation and word excel solution.

How to Use this Chapter in Business Valuation and Real Estate are source from Chapter 6 dealing on Investment Tools. Business valuation topic source comes from different courses in engineering, economics, finance and accounting. Undertakings and understanding are focused on formulas, its computation and applicability. It is a financially based approach analysis.

This book won't turn you into an expert overnight on critical business analysis impact or prepare you immediately, for the job of running an enterprise conglomerate. What it will do is to give results smoothly, efficient and effective with an educated reliability on decision making, tools you need to produce a sound result

Simply put, be a harbinger for a successful entrepreneurship that is allied to the business and real estate professions.

ACKNOWLEDGEMENT

"She, who is part of me, will always be the much better part."

A special thanks to my late **Dr. Febe Magsayo-Academia**, who together we created **MAGACA** and together we made a covenant to gift ourselves with eight blissfully wonderful kids, namely: Banjo, Beby, Gigi, Tenny, Monet, Jules Tommy, Em, Omar, Aim, Fides, Worly, Bebing, KC and Coy. Likewise, to my wondrous grand kids: TJ, AR, FM, Sam, Sash, Kyle, TomTom, Summer, Baby Banjo and Jacz. Most of the writing of this book is written in Muncie, Indiana. My host grandkids tennis and spelling bee regional champions, as well as, USA national spelling bee ranked competitors: SamSam and Sasha provided me with the impetus and tremendously inspired me to the highest level of my endeavor, ad infinitum.

SamSam – shifted sports interest from tennis to volleyball and back to tennis. In both sports she was at par-excellence in the group game even to the national school level competition, travelling around the USA. After an injury, she is back competing in tennis, and almost every day portion of time is allotted to a breathtaking tennis practice, what with the eagle's eye of her dad-coach direction. She simply superbly blew away all practices. And Sasha – magnificently fleet footed that glides so well in her tennis tournament.

I must write books as a contribution to the real estate finance and economics for a better decision making, sustainable development and adaptable environment for a wholesome humanity, by and large connectivity of mankind.

To Consultant, par excellent, who continue to inspire me, EVP Ampy Araullo, and the PARCS book author who gave me the insight to the mainstream of real estate consultancy practice-Chairman Doming the Vera. FIABCI Chairman Jun Dulalia, PAREB Presidents: Rey Lim and Emily Cabillada.

To my good friends Dr. Herbert Buot, Daisy Kokseng, Atty Amay Ong Vano and all others, though names not mentioned here, shall be embedded in my memory for a long, long time.

F9 Property Management and Consultants lead by Pres. Gerry Yangyang is a appreciated bond that keeps our corporate leadership efficiently continues to climb greater heights in the service of the real estate industry.

REAL ESTATE CONSULTANCY · DEVELOPMENT · MANAGEMENT · APPRAISAL · MARKETING · SALES

F9 Board of Directors
(Left to Right) Ma. Corazon A. de la Fuente, Rufilo L. Toledo, Gerardo B. Yangyang, Emily Amie L. Cabillada, Monina S. de la Calzada, Leticia B. Tauto-an, Caroline B. Borres, Jocelyn A. Jamero, Tomasito Z. Academia

To PAREB, what with its past and current management intricacies I learnt shall be kept as fresh memory to cherish, my heartfelt acknowledgement to you all.

Lastly, but never the least, to my Muncie, Indiana, USA, family-benefactor: Omar-Aimee who made the extra stride to keep me warm and comfortable, so with their love and care, to my two grandkids, who I am so proud to illustrate and elaborate on their academic and sports excellence. Sasha – 15 year old tennis and spelling bee champions: so graceful, consistent, diligent and smooth serving tennis buff, superb in many ways, SamSam at 16 years old a tennis power player has already travelled in many states for volleyball, tennis and spelling bee competitions. On January 2018 competition at Greentown, Indiana Tennis Tournament. Samantha emerged as champion for the 18 and under event – towering as Singles champion and Doubles champion with Sasha. With many upcoming sports and academic events, trophies, plaques, medals and certificates are abounding all over the house.

Congratulations goes to the father-coach Omar, as professional physical therapist, he is so stern sailor on a rough sea of his father-daughter coaching job. Aimee who sees to it that playing apparel is the best there is for her players, right food and supplement are consistently addressed right on. As a nurse, she manages that everything runs smoothly in the household.

In retrospect, Indiana is a U.S. state located in the Midwestern and Great Lakes regions of North America. Indiana is the 38th largest by area and the 17th most populous of the 50 United States. Its capital and largest city is Indianapolis. Indiana was admitted to the United States as the 19th U.S. state and home for the NBA Indiana Pacers.

Muncie, Indiana is an incorporated city and the seat of Delaware County, *Indiana*. It is located in East Central *Indiana*, about 50 miles (80 km) northeast of Indianapolis. The United States Census for 2010 reported the city's population was 70,085. It is the principal city of the *Muncie* metropolitan statistical area. https://en.wikipedia.org/wiki/Muncie,_Indiana

My boys (left to right):

Banjo-MBA-Entrepreneur

Worly-Civil Engineer-Church Builder

Tommy Jr.-Doctor of Dentistry-Currency Guro

Omar-Physical & Sports Therapist

TABLE OF CONTENTS

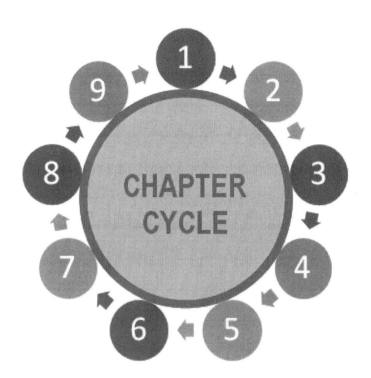

LEGEND:

Chapter 7 - Business Valuation

Chapter 8 – Business Etiquette and Protocol

Chapter 9 - Real Estate Consultancy

This course guidebook is meant to be learnt and learn again as a course guidebook cycle. This is the hierarchy of learning the theory and practice in the realm of real estate and business industries. The author spent a good number of years from 1988 to 1996 in the practice of real estate in Los Angeles, California but accumulated a vast number of years practice in the Philippines. Most of the writings of this book were written in Muncie, Indiana. However, dominant illustrations and sample are of Philippine settings.

On why you need this book – you may already know and believe that there is a scarcity of books in real estate that is home grown and of local authors, we encourage each other to dedicate and make available of their talents henceforth and come forward to write and publish books.

You can have the best idea, the best product and the best plan but if this is not communicated and made available to others, then you could end up less fulfilled. No one guarantees that your idea is transformative but the impact along the way is much appreciated sooner than expected.

CHAPTERS PREVIEW

INTRODUCTION

Congratulations on your desire to have a reference book on business and real estate in your hands. The huge emerging pace we are experiencing in the realm of finance, economics, engineering, environment, development and technology is unprecedented. Would we have a choice but cope up? It is worth to keep abreast on the basics of mathematic\al science encompassing our everyday challenges.

Let me underscore the theory of "back to the basics." When all things get complicated – simplify. And for this reason even arithmetic is being touched here, onward to geometrical and exponential to logarithm are emphasized too.

Many start-up developers, the likes of F9 Property Management Consultancy aggressively ventured into building constructions and development. Thanks to all F9ners, for so many years of business bonding we are there to have and get it through. My objective was to make this material accessible for the general users and service these needs in one way or the other.

Many companies, my peers, middle managements, financial and economics students and professionals would like to have a reference on hand to augment knowledge on this area.

Suggestion on the use of this book:

Browse on a particular subject you want attention

Detailed study is from the beginning of the chapter to the last

Have fun along the way, absorb the knowledge and enjoy.

Much of the complexity of any undertaking is always the toughness of the subject you want to study, whenever you feel that way, simplify – by focusing on a particular topic and take it from there one subject matter at a time.

Read and study for key details - big ideas need support. Otherwise they're just opinions. After you identify each big idea, make note of the supporting details that fill out and help the big idea make sense.

Find time for adjustment in your comprehension on any chosen subject before being able to read a whole chapter.

The investment tools presented on chapter six is a good focal point to go to especially on a research you may be undertaking.

At the end of the day! The consultancy defines outcome

Consultant-Messenger –

MESSAGE

- Client-Receiver

HAPTER ONE

BUSINESS PLAN OUTLINE

"If you're not prepared to be wrong, you'll never come up with anything original"

- Ken Robinson

I. OBJECTIVE, PURPOSE AND APPROACH

➤ *To learn what it is all about Business Plan Outline*

➤ *To establish an environment conducive to studying and learning.*

➤ *To identify opportunity cost on time and effort spent*

➤ *To strategize planning and management both on long term and now*

➤ *To introduce delivery skills for a successful quality services to clients*

After this chapter:

You will know the basic concept and criteria in the preparation of business Plan.

Use the Applicability Theory of **MOST**: **M**ission and **O**bjectives on <u>what</u> a business company is seeking to do. **S**trategy and **T**actics is on <u>how</u> a business enterprise or company will achieve it.

II. Executive Summary

An executive summary should not be more than two pages, but without sacrificing quality: According to the **7 Cs**, communication needs to be:

- Clear

- Concise

- Concrete

- Correct

- Coherent

- Complete

- Courteous

that will succinctly serve as an overview of your entire business plan and emphasize the key issues to be had. Highlight all concerns that must be your company's distinctive competence. Show the issues of competence and advantage your business will deal on the challenges for success in a competitive market.

A. The Purpose of the Plan

1. Stakeholder's appreciation

2. Emphasis on return of investment

3. Includes Technical and Operational plan

4. Decision-making tool

B. Market Analysis

1. Shows its geographic and demographic target area

2. Clients satisfaction of product or services offered

C. Company Profile

1. Shows how your company will satisfy

2. Product satisfaction information

D. Sales Activities

1. Market penetration strategy

2. Sales strategy

3. Keys and hold on competitive environment

E. Research and Development

1. Continues upgrade

2. Major milestone

F. Organization Set up

1. Personnel

2. Technical employees

3. Owners

4. Stakeholders

G. Financial Data

1. Funds requirement annually, short and long term

2. History and financial summary

3. Financial, justification and satisfaction summary

H. Legal Aspect

1. Government mandate

2. Cost of doing business

3. Local regulations

I. Socio-Economics

1. Community Involvement

2. Level of participation

3. Services Involvement

J. Environmental-Cultural

1. Serves for a better community

2. Environment friendly standard

III. Market Analysis: through the maximization use of the theory of **SWOT** framework that can evaluate a company.

1. **Strength** – positive internal attribute

2. **Weakness** – any negative internal attribute

3. **Opportunities** – the advantages of external environment for growth

4. **Threat** – negative impact from any externalities

The Market Analysis section should reflect your knowledge of your industry, and present highlights and analysis of your market research. It provides basis for prospective sales and pricing estimates. This is a test of your ability to communicate the essence of your business. You must be certain that this section concisely and accurately describes the substance of your new business.

A. Industry Description and Outlook

1. Description of your primary industry

2. Size of the industry

    a). Past Performance

    b). Currently

    c). In short terms of three years

    d). In long terms of five to ten years

3. Industry characteristics and market trends

    a). Past trends

    b). Current Indicators

    c). Future project and Expectation

4. Major customer groups

   a). Businesses

   b). Governments

   c). Public

   d). Suppliers

B. Target Markets

1. Differentiation of characteristics of primary target markets

   a). Special and typical needs

   b). Extent and size to which those needs are being met

   c). Demographic segmentation

   d). Geographic location

   e). Buying decision-makers and consumers

   f). Seasonal/cyclical trends

2. Primary/target market size.

   a). Number of prospective customers.

   b). Annual purchases of products or services

   c). Geographic area.

   d). Market anticipation

3. Market penetration: extent and size to which you anticipate penetrating the market and demonstrate why you feel that level of penetration is achievable based on your market research

   a). Market share

b). Number of customers

c). Geographic coverage

d). Market penetration estimates

4. Pricing/gross margin targets

   a). Price levels

   b). Gross margin levels

   c). Percent Discount structure

5. Methods on specific numbers of your target market can be identified

   a). Directories

   b). Trade association publications

   c). Government documents

6. Communication media to specific members of your target market

   a). Publications

   b). Radio/television broadcasts

   c). Sources of influence/advice

   d). Internet

7. Purchasing cycle of potential customers

   a). Needs identification

   b). Research for solutions to needs

   c). Solution evaluation process

   d). Final solution selection responsibility and authority

8. Primary and secondary target markets and key attributes

    a). Needs

    b). Demographics

    c). Significant future trends

C. Market Test Results

1. Potential customers contacted.

2. Information/demonstrations given to potential customers.

3. Reaction of potential customers.

4. Importance of satisfaction of targeted needs.

5. Price market willingness test to purchase products/services.

D. Distribution Lead Times of product or services delivery

1. Initial orders

2. Reorders

3. Volume purchases

E. Competition

1. Identification of product or service and its market segment

    a). Existing

    b). Market share

   c). Potential product sustainability on how to handle competition

   d). Direct

   e). Indirect

2. Strengths - Theory of **SMART**: <u>S</u>pecific in focusing a project at a time, <u>M</u>easurable on the expected deliverables, <u>A</u>ttainable, notwithstanding sky is the limit. It is <u>R</u>elevant to the insight of expectations, and limited variance and scope of its <u>Time</u> framed.

   a). Ability to satisfy customer needs

   b). Market penetration

   c). Track record and reputation

   d). Staying power (financial resources)

   e). Key personnel

3. Weaknesses – Theory of **SMART**

   a). Ability to satisfy customer needs

   b). Market penetration

   c). Track record and reputation

   d). Staying power (financial resources)

   e). Key personnel

4. Importance of your target market to your competition

5. Barriers to entry into the market

   a). Capital investment

   b). Time

   c). Technology

d). Key personnel

e). Customer treads

f). Existing patents and trademarks

g). Regulatory Restrictions

IV. Company Description

This shows how all of the elements of your company fit together without going into detail.

1. Nature of Your Business

   a). Marketplace needs to be satisfied

   b). Methods of satisfaction and needs

   c). Individuals/organizations with the needs

2. Your Company's Distinctive Competencies

   a). Superior customer needs satisfaction

   b). Product delivery efficiencies

   c). Personnel

   d). Geographic location

V. Marketing and Sales Activities

The objective here is to describe the activities that will allow you to meet the sales and margin levels indicated in your prospective financial statements.

A. Overall Marketing Strategy

1. Marketing penetration strategy

2. Growth strategy

    a). Internal

    b). Acquisition

    c). Franchise

    d). Horizontal product to different users.

    e). Vertical product to different levels of distribution chain

3. Distribution channels include discount and profitability

    a). Original equipment manufacturers

    b). Internal sales force

    c). Distributors

    d). Retailers

4. Communication

    a). Promotion

    b). Advertising business

    c). Public relations

    d). Personal selling

    e). Printed materials

B. Sales Strategies

1. Sales force

    a). Analyze advantage and disadvantages strategy.

    b). Size

    c). Recruitment and training

    d). Compensation

2. Sales activities

    a). Identifying prospects

    b). Prioritizing prospects

    c). Number of sales calls made per period

    d). Average number of sales calls per sale

    e). Average dollar size per sale

    f). Average dollar size per reorder

VI. Products and Services

Special attention should be paid to the users of your business plan.

A. Detailed Product/Service Description

1. Specific benefits of product/service

2. Ability to meet needs

3. Competitive advantages

4. Present stage (idea, prototype, small production runs, etc.)

B. Product Life Cycle

1. Description of the product/service's current position in its life cycle

2. Factors that might change the anticipated life cycle

    a). Lengthen it

    b). Shorten it

C. Intangibles

1. Existing or pending copyrights or patents

2. Anticipated copyright and patent filings

3. Aspects of products or services that cannot be patented or copyrighted

4. Key aspects of your products or services that qualify as trade secrets

5. Existing legal agreements with owners and employees

    a). Nondisclosure agreements

    b). Incomplete agreements

D. Research and Development Activities

1. Activities in process

2. Future activities - included then and now

3. Anticipated results of future research and development activities

   a). New products or services

   b). New generations of existing products or services

   c). Complementary products or services

   d). Replacement products or services

4. Research and development activities of others in your industry

   a). Direct competitors

   b). Indirect competitors

   c). Suppliers

   d). Customers

VII. Operations

These are some basic questions that must be dealt with from top to bottom and bottom to top management included in the matrix of operation. The participants and stakeholders must be duly knowledgeable of everyone involvement in its business operation and management.

   a). What is a business management operation all about?

   b). What is a functional business management meant?

   c). What system does it takes to follow operation processes?

   d). What do daily monitoring operations system mean?

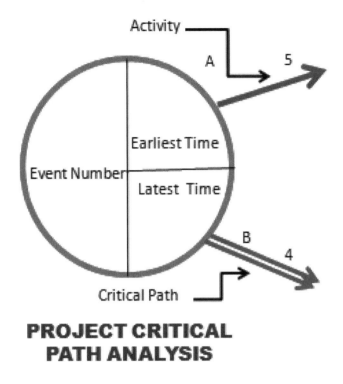

PROJECT CRITICAL
PATH ANALYSIS

Here again, too much detail can detract from the rest of your plan.

Be certain that the level of details included fits the specific needs of the plan's users. Principle: network analysis is a technique for planning big projects by programming and monitoring growth.

PERT - **P**roject **E**valuation and **R**eview Technique is a form of network analysis

1. **Project Activity** A – follows the normal flow to the project

2. **Critical Path B** – where adjustment is made, either finance, technical operation or negative economic trend.

a). Contingency cash flow inadequacy

b). Technical operation staff migrated

c). Peso-dollar imbalance equivalency

d). Political-environmental changes

3. Earliest time or ahead of schedule

4. Latest time or delayed of schedule

5. Organization event number

1. Production and Service Delivery Procedures

    a). Internal

    b). External - contractors/subcontractors

2. Production and Service Delivery Capability

    a). Internal

    b). External - Suppliers

    c). Anticipated increases in capacity

    d). Investment

    e). New cost factors - direct and indirect

    f). Timing

3. Operating Competitive Advantages

    a). Techniques

    b). Experience

    c). Economies of scale

    d). Lower direct costs

4. Suppliers

    a). Identification of the suppliers of critical elements of production

    b). Primary

    c). Secondary

    d). Lead - time requirements

    e). Evaluation of the risks of critical element shortages

VIII. Management and Ownership

Emphasize the strength of the management team as business competencies.

1. Management Staff Structure

    a). Management staff organizational chart

    b). Narrative description of the chart

2. Key Managers resumes.

    a). Name

    b). Position

    c). Brief position description, including primary duties

    d). Primary responsibilities and authority

    e). Skills and experiences unique to your company's competencies

    f). Compensation basis and levels

3. Planned Additions to the Current Management Team

    a). Position

    b). Primary responsibilities and authority

    c). Requisite skills and experience

    d). Recruitment process

    e). Timing of employment

    f). Anticipated contribution to the company's success

    g). Compensation basis and levels in line with the market

IX. Funds Required and its Uses

Any new or additional findings reflected in your prospective financial statements should be discussed here.

1. Current Funding Requirements

    a). Amount

    b). Timing

    c). Expected funding needed over the next three to five years

2. Type

    a). Equity

    b). Debt

    c). Terms

3. Use of Funds

    a). Capital expenditures

b). Working capital

c). Debt retirement

d). Acquisitions

X. Financial Data

This is an area where specialized knowledge can be so invaluable. The Financial Data section contains the financial representations of all the information presented.

1. Historical Financial Data

2. Annual statements

   a). Income

   b). Balance sheet

   c). cash flow

3. Prospective Financial Data

   a). Income

   b). Balance sheet

   c). Cash flows

   d). Capital expenditure budget

4. Historical financial statements

   a). Ratio analysis

   b). Trend analysis with graphic presentation

5. Prospective financial statements

   a). Ratio analysis

b). Trend analysis with graphic presentation

6. Appendices or Exhibits

    a). Any additional detailed data that is useful to the readers.

    b). Resumes of Key Managers

    c). Pictures of Products

    d). Professional References

    e). Market Studies

7. Significant Contracts

    a). Leases

    b). Sales contracts

    c). Purchase contracts

8. Partnership/ownership agreements

    a). Stock option agreements

    b). Employment/compensation agreements

9. Incomplete agreements

    a). Insurance

    b). Product liability

10. Officers' and directors' liability

11. General liability

XI. Standard Tables and Charts

For clarity, provide business tables and charts in the standard business plan. Also, include bar charts and pie charts to illustrate the numbers

1. Cash flow

2. Sales Forecast and Profit and Loss statements

3. Projected Balance sheet

4. Projected Business Ratios, and Market Analysis tables

hapter One

XII. Assessment:

This Business Plan Outline is arrays of chapter summary templates.

The financiers, investors or funders may first a look what may be offered in the table in the chapter assessment.

Compiling numerous sets of data into few pages as highlighted here. Remember when to be a specialist or a generalist in the enterprise undertaking you are involved with before your prospective clients.

A company can make the whole process a breeze and impeccably efficient and it will not only provide a clear picture to the investor but also reduce the expenditure. Remember it consists of three main sections namely executive summary along with company, products, and services and profitability.

1. **Long-term goal of strategy.** What an organization is and wants to become

2. **Total Quality Management (TQM)** is concerned with quality right throughout the organization, not just at the production stage.

3. **Ongoing program of activity** which is designed to help an organization or an individual achieves goals and objectives. A corporate strategy can be evaluated on six basic criteria: Internal consistency;

4. **Environment Management System** - Consistent with what must good for the environment; Appropriateness in the light of available resources; an acceptable degree of risk; an appropriate time horizon; feasibility of the strategy.

5. **Pareto Principle** - In any 'normal' situation it is found that approximately 20% of items account for 80% of the effect.

XIII. Academia Maxima – The Eight P Plan

ACADEMIA MAXIMA
(THE 8 P PLAN)-Dr. Tomasito Z. Academia
HOW TO STRATEGIZE ENTERPRISE

PLAN PURPOSELY

PREPARE PRAYERFULLY

PROCEED POSITIVELY

PURSUE PERSISTENTLY

PERSEVERE PAINSTAKINGLY

POTENTIALS & POSSIBILITIES

PRESENT PERSUASIVELY

PROTECT AND PRESERVE

Over the years of real estate practice, I come to the conclusion and developed a way of life –a mantra: "less is more". The **academia-maxima or the eight p plan** becomes my guiding post in life as a beacon that focuses and search, a full and wide panorama view or even a 360 – degree appreciation that is aligned to the virtues of the true needs of an enterprise, desires and wants in everyone's life.

The heights scaled by great men attained and kept are likened into a learning curve, sometimes slow, but other times fast and progressive, primordially fundamental no matter how slow - it is moving.

HAPTER TWO

BASIC MATHEMATICS

Life is like riding a bicycle. To keep your balance, you must keep moving.
Albert Einstein

I. OBJECTIVE, PURPOSE AND APPROACH

➤ *To establish an environment conducive for study and learning*

➤ *To learn what it is all about real estate practice to basic math*

➤ *To allow the opportunity to identify on time and effort spent*

➤ *To introduce the professional skills necessary to be successful*

After this chapter, you will have learned:

❖ *You will know the basic concept of real estate math for an interesting and understanding problems solving as a critical tools for thorough analysis

❖ How to present to business clients different financial comparative approaches to make

❖ How to knowledgeably sell or persuade and convince your clients on the service or product you present.

II. Fraction

Common Fraction - a rational number written as an ordered pair of integers, called the numerator and denominator. The denominator cannot be zero.

Proper Fraction - if the absolute value of the numerator is less than the absolute value of the denominator - the value of the entire fraction is < 1.

Improper Fraction - If the absolute value of the numerator is greater than or equal to the absolute value of the denominator > 1, that is 7/5

Mixed number - The sum of a whole number and a proper fraction, the whole and fractional parts of the number are written: 2 + 3/4 = 2 3/4

An improper fraction is another way to write a whole plus a part.

A mixed number can be converted to an improper fraction as follows:

Example: The sum of 2 3/4 = 8/4 + 3/4 = 11 / 4

11/4, divide 11 by 4. 11 ÷ 4 = 2 with remainder 3.

If the quotient is with a remainder, then becomes the whole number part of the mixed number.

Reciprocal of a fraction is another fraction with the numerator and denominator reversed.

Example: 3/7, for instance, is 7/3.

The product of a fraction and its reciprocal is 1. Hence, the reciprocal is the multiplicative inverse of a fraction. Any integer can be written as a fraction

Example: 17 can be written as 17/1, where 1 is sometimes referred to as the unseen denominator. The reciprocal of 17 is 1/17.

Complex fractions

In a complex fraction, either the numerator, or the denominator, or both, is a fraction or a mixed number.

Example: 1/2 divide by 1/3:

1/2

—— = 1/2 x 3/1 = 3/2 = 1 1/2

1/3

Example: 2/3 divided by 5 is complex fractions.

2/3

—— = 3/2 x 1/5 = 3/10

5

Example: 8 divide by 1/3

$$\frac{8}{1/3} = 8 \times 3/1 = 24$$

Compound fractions

Example: 3/4 x 5/7 = 15/28

Decimal fractions and percentages

4.75 can be written either as an improper fraction, 475/100, or as a mixed number, 4 75/100

Decimal fractions can also be expressed using scientific notation with negative exponents, such as 5.023×10^{-6}, which represents 0.000005023. The 10^{-6} represents a denominator of 10^6. Dividing by 10^6 moves the decimal point 6 steps to the left. Thus 85% means 85/100.

Arithmetic with fractions

Fractions obey the commutative, associative, and distributive laws, and the rule against division by zero.

Addition: The first rule of addition is that only like quantities can be added

Example: 2/4 + 3/4 = 1 1/4

Adding unlike quantities: For adding quarters to thirds, both types of fraction are converted to $1/4 \times 1/3 = 1/12$

Consider adding the following two quantities: Now it can be seen that:

$3/4 + 2/3 = 9/12 + 8/12 = 17/12 = 1\ 5/12$

This method can be expressed algebraically: $a/b + c/d = (ad + cb)/bd$

Subtraction: The resulting fraction will have that denominator, and its numerator will be the result of subtracting the numerators of the original fractions.

Example: $2/3 - 1/2 = 4/6 - 3/6 = 1/6$

Multiplication: To multiply fractions, multiply the numerators and multiply the denominators.

Example: $2/3 \times 3/4 = 6/12$

A two is a common factor in both the numerator of the left fraction and the denominator of the right and is divided out of both. Three is a common factor of the left denominator and right numerator and is divided out of both.

Multiplying a fraction by a whole number

Example: $6 \times 3/4 = 18/4$

This method works because the fraction 6/1 means six equal parts, each one of which is a whole.

Mixed numbers

When multiplying mixed numbers, it's best to convert the mixed number into an improper fraction.

Example: 3 x 2 3/4 = 3 x (8/4 + 3/4) = 3 x 11/4 = 33/4 = 8 1/4

Division

Example: (10/3) /5 = 10 / 15 = 2/3

Formulas for the arithmetic of fractions

Example: Again, Let *a, b, c, d* be positive integers.

$$\frac{a}{b} + \frac{c}{d} = \frac{ad + bc}{bd} \qquad \frac{a}{b} - \frac{c}{d} = \frac{ad - bc}{bd} \qquad \frac{a}{b} \div \frac{c}{d} = \frac{ad}{bc}$$

Two fractions can be compared using the rule **a/b>c/d** if and only if *ad > bc.* Two fractions **a/b and c/d** are equivalent if and only if

ad = bc.

Dividing Fractions by Fractions

Example: Divide 2/9 and 3/12 = 24/27 = 8/9

Dividing Fractions by Whole Numbers

Example: Divide 2/9 by 2 = 2/18 = 1/9

Dividing Mixed Numbers

Example: 6 2/8 ÷ 3 5/9 = 50/8 ÷ 32/9 = 450/256 = 1 194/256

Multiplying Fractions

Example: Multiply 2/9 and 3/12 6/108 = 1/18

Multiplying Mixed Numbers

Example: 6 2/8 x 3 5/9 = 50/8 x 32/9 1600/72 = 22 16/72

= 22 2/9

Fractions and Equivalent Decimals

Example: 0.1 and 1/10 0.2 and 1/5 0.5 and 1/2 0.25 and 1/4

0.50 and 1/2 0.75 and 3/4 1.0 and 1/1 or 2/2 or 1

Square Roots - Terms for raising a number to the 2nd power. Example:

$2^2 = 4.$	Read as 2 squared equals 4.	Means that 2 x 2 = 4
$3^3 = 9.$	Read as 3 squared equals 9.	Means that 3 x 3 = 9
$4^4 = 16.$	Read as 4 squared equals 16.	Means that 4 x 4 = 16

Taking the "square root" is the opposite of squaring a number! Example:

$2^2 = 4$	opposite is	$\sqrt{4} = 2$
2 squared = 4	square root of	4 = 2

The most common square roots

$2^2 = 4$	2.2 = 4	$\sqrt{4} = 2$	What number times itself = 4?
$3^2 = 9$	3.3 = 9	$\sqrt{9} = 3$	What number times itself = 9?
$4^2 = 16$	4.4 = 16	$\sqrt{16} = 4$	What number times itself = 16?
$5^2 = 25$	5.5 = 25	$\sqrt{25} = 5$	What number times itself = 25?
$6^2 = 36$	6.6 = 36	$\sqrt{36} = 6$	What number times itself = 36?
$7^2 = 49$	7.7 = 49	$\sqrt{49} = 7$	What number times itself = 49?
$8^2 = 64$	8.8 = 64	$\sqrt{64} = 8$	What number times itself = 64?
$9^2 = 81$	9.9 = 81	$\sqrt{81} = 9$	What number times itself = 81?

The expression √4 only is the positive square root of 4, which is

√4 = 2

If you want the negative square root, then you must use a negative sign (outside of the square root symbol -√4 = -2

If you want a negative square root, the negative sign must be outside of the radical sign.

Example: 6 x 6 =36, so the answer is positive

-(6)(-6) = 36, and the answer is positive

III. Ratio and Proportion

Solve proportions by ratios as fractions, setting the two fractions equal to each other, cross-multiplying, and solving the resulting equation:

Problem 1 – X is the unknown value in the proportion 2 : X

= 3 : 9

Then, 2 / X = 3 / 9 9 (2) = X (3) 18 = 3X 6 = X

Problem 2 – A developer wants to service the highly urbanized city needs of dwelling units in Cebu. Currently every 24 housing unit detached has to balance on condominium units need of 400. But a huge demand backlog is being experienced due to influx and surge of housing requirements from different areas in Visayas and Mindanao. From data gathered a need of 36 residential must be supplied, correspondingly, how many condo units must be supplied to balance the market requirement?

Given: 24 : 400   36 : X

$$\frac{24}{400} = \frac{36}{X} = 600, \text{ hence, there are units of condo needed}$$

or a ratio of 1.5

Problem 3 – The tax on a property with an assessed value of P700,000 is P11,000. What is the value of a property if the tax is P14,000?

$$\frac{700,000}{11,000} = \frac{V}{14,000} = V = \text{Value} = \text{P890,090.91}$$

IV. Percent

Percent means parts per hundred with a percent symbol %. To calculate the percentage increase: First: work out the difference between the two comparing numbers. Then, divide Difference by the original number and multiply the answer by 100 %.

Problem 1- What percent of 20 is 30? $30 = (X)(20)$

$30 \div 20 = X = 1.5$ 1.5 x 100 = 150%

Problem 2 - What is 35% of 80?

$X = (0.35)(80)$ $X = 28 = 35\%$ of 80

Problem 3 - 45% of what is 12?

$12 = (45\%)\,(X)$

$12 = 0\ 45$ of (X)

$X = 26.67$

Problem 4 - A payment is made at P60.95. The total bill is P70.61.

What is its city tax rate.

$70.61 - 60.95 = 9.66$

$9.66 = (X)(60.95)$

$(X) = 0.1585$ x $100 = 15.85\%$

Sales tax paid is 15.85%.

Problem 5 - An original sale price is P175 a kilogram but lately increased to P205 81 per kg. What is its percent increase?

$205.81 - 175 = 30.81$

$30.81\ /\ 175 = 0.1761$ or 17.61% increase

Percentage Problems

Problem 1: An original price of a shirt was P200. It was decreased to P150. What is the percent decrease of the price of this shirt? The decrease is 200 -150 =P50. The percent decrease is the absolute decrease divided by the original price (part / whole). % decease

= 50 / 200 = 0.25

% decrease = 25 / 100 = 25%

Problem 2: She has a monthly salary of P12,000. She spends P2,800 per month on food. What percent of her monthly salary does she spend on food?

%= part / whole = 2800 / 12000 = 0.23

% = 0.23 x 100= 23%

Problem 3: The price of a mango fruit was decreased by 22% to $300. What was the original price of the fruit? Let x be the original price

Let y be the absolute decrease The price was decreased to $300

then,

X - Y = 300 Y is given by

Y = 22% of X = (22 / 100) * x = 0.22 X

X - 0.22 X = 30 0.78 X = 30 X = P380.5

Problem 4: The price of an item changed from P1200 to 1000. Then later the price decreased again from P1000 to P800. Which of the two decreases was larger in percentage term?

1st part / whole = (1200 - 1000) / 1200 = 0.17 = 17%

2nd part / whole = (1000 - 800) / 1000 = 0.20 = 20%

Therefore, the second decrease was larger in percent term. The parts were the same in both cases but the whole was smaller in the second decrease.

Problem 5: The price of an item decreased by 20% to P2000, then later the price decreased again from P2000 to 1500. What is the percent of decrease from the original price to the final price of 1500? We first need to find the original price x. The first decrease gives

X - 20% X = 2000 0.8 X = 2000

X = 2000 / 0.8 = 2500

The percentage decrease from the original price 2500 to 1500 is given by part / whole = (250 - 150) / 250 = 0.4 = 40%

Problem 6: A number increases from 300 to 400 and then decreases from 400 to 300. Compare the percent of increase from 300 to 400 and that of the decrease from 400 to 300. Percent increase from 300 to 400 is given by

(400 - 300) / 300 = 100 / 300 = 0.33 = 33%

Percent decrease from 40 to 30 is given by

(400 - 300) / 400 = 0.25 = 25%

In absolute term, the percent decrease is less than the percent increase.

Problem 7: A family had dinner in a restaurant and paid P3000 for food. They also had to pay 9.5% sale tax and 10% for the tip. How much did they pay for the dinner? They paid for food, sales tax and tip, hence, the total paid = P3000 + 9.5% * 3000 + 10% * 3000

= P3,585

Problem 8: A shop is offering discounts on shirts costing P200 each. If someone buys 2 shirts, he will be offered a discount of 15% on the first shirt and another 10% discount on the reduced price for the second shirt. How much would one pay for two shirts at this shop?

The reduced price for the first shirt

200 - 15% * 200 = P170

170 - 10% * 170 = P153

170 + 153 = P323 Cost for the two shirts

Problem 9: Ruffy invested P50,000 for two years. For the first year, the rate of interest was 7% and the second year it was 8.5%. How much interest earned at the end of the two year period?

Interest at the end of the 1ST first year 7% * 50,000 = P3500

Interest at the end of the 2ND year 8.5% * (50000 + 3500)

= P4547.50

Total interest end of the two year period is 3500 + P4547.5

= P8047.50

Problem 9: In 2017 our world population is 6.8 billion. 25% of which lives in Developed Countries (DC) with a Population Growth Rate (PGR) of 1.50%. and 75% of the total population lives in the Less Developed Countries (LDC) with a PGR of 2.50%. What is our planet earth population by year 2022?

Solution: 6.8B x 25% = 1.7B lives in DC

6.8B x 75% = 5.1B lives LDC

DC = $1.7 (1 + .15)^5 = 1,831,382,800$

LDC = $5.1 (1 + .025)^5 = 5,770,181,800$

World Population by 2022 = 7,601,564,600

Problem 14: Worly has a fixed monthly salary of P5,000 with an incentive of 5% of all monthly sales. What should his sales be so his take home pay for the month reaches P15,000?

$15,000 = 5,000 + 5\% \times X = 500 + 0.05 X$

$X = (15000 - 5000) / 0.05 = P200,000$

V. Exponent and Logarithm

Rule # 1 – Multiply Powers with the same base only.

Add the exponents. Example: X^a x $X^b = X^{a+b}$ X^3 x X^5 equals X^8

Rule #2 – Raising a Power to a Power with different bases.

Multiply the exponents Example: $(X^a)^b = X^{ab}$

When multiplying powers with the same base, add the exponents

Rule # 3 – Power of a Product Property

Find the power of each factor and multiply Example: $(XY)^a$

$= X^a Y^a$

Rule # 4 – Negative Integer Exponents

Rewrite the power as an equivalent expression with a positive exponent by taking the reciprocal

Example:

$$X^{-a} = \frac{1}{X^a}$$

Comparative and equivalent - Similar rules for exponential and logarithms.

$b^y = X$ is called exponential	$Y = \log_b x$ is called logarithm
$2^{-1} = 1/2$	$\log_2(1/2) = -1$
$2^0 = 1$	$\log_2(1) = 0$
$2^1 = 2$	$\log_2(2) = 1$
$2^2 = 4$	$\log_2(4) = 2$
$2^3 = 8$	$\log_2(8) = 3$
$2^4 = 16$	$\log_2(16) = 4$
$4^2 = 16$	$\log_4(16) = 2$

Log Rules:

1. $\log_b(mn) = \log_b(m) + \log_b(n)$

2. $\log_b(^m/_n) = \log_b(m) - \log_b(n)$

3. $\log_b(m^n) = n\log_b(m)$

Log rules as expressed:

1. Multiplication inside the log can be turned into addition outside the log, and vice versa.

2. Division inside the log can be turned into subtraction outside the log, and vice versa.

3. An exponent on everything inside a log can be moved out front as a multiplier, and vice versa.

hapter Two

VI. Assessment

This Basic Math is arrays of chapter summary templates. To the students, professionals, bankers, lenders and investors: Should something hampers our decision on basic mathematical approaches; let us just visit our undertakings in this chapter. On fractions Ratio and proportion, percent problems, exponents and logarithms and numerous compilation sets of test problems are being presented in this chapter here.

If you don't drive your business, you will be driven out of business. – B. C. Forbes (Founder of Forbes)

This is a proverbial slogan that stands the test of time. The company can make the whole process a breeze with impeccable efficiency and a clearer and bigger business picture

Remember when anything stares to be wrong; go back to the mathematical basic then continue and dissect the critical and analytical conditions before you.

"Life is a math equation. In order to gain the most, you have to know how to convert negatives into positives." – Anonymous. And according to **Andrew Wiles** - "Just because we can't find a solution it doesn't mean that there isn't one." In one way or the other, there is a good solution. But wait there could be a better answer. Let us find it!

Do what you can, with what you have, where you are and people excel and learn, not because they are told to, but because they want to.

Business methodology must continue to be explored and discovery of the vast oceans of opportunity will be just closer as you can imagine and learn the rules so you know how to vigorously pursue them properly.

Before anything else, basic mathematics is simply a tool for the bigger picture of our profession and on what we want to accomplish as a real estate broker- the important business cog in real estate industry; real estate appraiser – valuing properties and business enterprise; real estate consultant – giving advices and doing consulting for a fee; and not the least as an environmental planner – seeing to it that the real estate industry stakeholders must always remember we do things in mind to live a legacy and posterity for the next generations after us.

CHAPTER THREE

SIMPLE INTEREST
AND DISCOUNT

"Whoever renders service to many put himself in line for greatness - great wealth, great return, great satisfaction, great reputation, and great joy". - **Jim Rohn**

I. OBJECTIVE, PURPOSE AND APPROACH

- ➤ *To establish an environment conducive for study and learning.*

- ➤ *To learn what all about basic math applicable to real estate practice*

- ➤ *To allow the opportunity to identify on time and effort spent*

- ➤ *To introduce the life skills necessary to be successful in quality services*

After this chapter, you will have learned:

- ❖ Review and learn the keystone concepts, theories and practices concerning basic business math, and through governing fund management

- ❖ Understand the external and intrinsic factors that impact of theorem and real business practice.

❖ Acquire the requisite fundamental and technical tools for investment decision-making

❖ Think critically about how theory and practice interact in the real the real estate industry

❖ Apply your learned competencies in creating a fund, designing its strategy defend your investment outcome

❖ Gain knowledge and skill that adds value to your financial or investments.

II. Interest

Interest. - The payment made for use of money over a period of time. The interest is computed on the original principal during the whole time at the stated interest rate.

Discount. - The difference of money from the maturity value of an obligation when the before its due date or date of maturity. It is a percentage of the amount or maturity value and not a percentage of the principal.

III. Formula

FORMULA : Simple Interest

$I = Prt$

$P = I / rt$

$r = I / Pt$

$t = I / Pr$

$F = P + I$

$F = P(1 + rt)$

NOTATIONS

I = Simple Interest

P = Principal, Face Value, Present Value

r = rate of interest

t = time (in years or fractional parts)

F = Final Amount

Io = Ordinary Interest

I_e = Exact Interest

D = Simple Discount

d = discount rate

Simple Interest I = F - P

Simple Interest formulas when t is expressed in days

$I_{o=}$ Pr number of days - as the banker's Rule 360

$I_{e=}$ Pr number of days divided by 365

IV. Simple Discount

D = Fdt

d = D/Ft

F = D/dt

D = F - P

t = D/Fd

Present Value

P = F - D

or

P = F(1-dt)

Simple Interest rate - as equivalent to a given Simple Discount rate

R = d /1-dt

Simple Discount rate - as equivalent to a given Simple Interest rate

d = /1 + rt

To discount F for t years at simple discount rate d, use

D = Fdt

then

P = F - D

At simple interest rate r, use

P = F /(1 + rt)

Example 1:

1. Jay owed P5,000 from Banjo on March 23, 2017 and promised to pay the principal plus simple interest at 9% and pay debt on December 18, 2017. How much shall he pay upon maturity date?

Solution:

Use the Banker's Rule to find simple interest as implied.

Actual no. of days

December - 12/18 = 352

March -   03/23 = -82

              = 270 days

Simple Interest by the Banker's Rule

I_o = Pr Actual no. of days divided by 360

   = (5,000) (.09) 270

   = 337.50

Amount to be paid on maturity date

F = P + I

   = P5,000 + 337.50

   = P5,337.50

Example 2

Bring in P12,500 for 2 years and 6 months with 9% simple interest.

Simple Interest I = Prt

Solution: (P12,500)(.09)(2.5)

= P2,812.50

Final Amount   **F = P + I**

= P12,500.00 + P2,812.50

= 15,312.50

Example 3:

Discount P9,700 for 30 days at

a). 8% simple interest

b). 8% simple discount

Solution:

a). P = F / (1 + rt)

= P9,700 / 1 + (.08) 30/ 360

= P9,635.76

b). I = Fdt

= (P9,700)(.08) 30/360

= P64.67

$P = F - I$

$= P9,700 - P64.67$

$= P9,635.33$

Example 4:

Monet's in her time deposit at PNB is P60,000. The bank gave him 16% for a term of 30 days. There is a 15% withholding tax to be deducted from the interest. a) How much is his withholding tax? b) How much net interest will he receive?

a). I = Prt

$= (60,000)(.16)\ 30/360$

$= P800$

Withholding Tax

$= I \times .15$

$= P800 \times .15$

$= P120.00$

b). Net Interest

$= \text{Interest} - \text{Withholding Tax}$

= P800 - P120

= P680

Table 1 – Formula used in compounding and discounting approaches all throughout this guidebook. This presentation is to familiarize us in its uses.

V. Comparative formula presentation

BUSINESS	ENGINEERING
$S^n = (1 + i)^n$	$FV = 1 (1 + i)^n$
$1/s^n = 1/(1 + i)^n$	$PV = FV (1 + i)^{-n}$
$S_{n\rceil i} = (S^n - 1) / i$	$FV = pmt [(1 + i)^n - 1] / i$
$1/S_{n\rceil} = i / S^n - 1$	$pmt = FV [i / (1 + i)^n - 1]$
$A_{n\rceil} = (1 - 1/S^n) / i$	$PV = pmt [1-(1 + i)^{-n}] /i$
$1/ A_{n\rceil} = i / (1 - 1/S^n)$	$pmt = PV [i /1-(1 + i)^{-n}]$

VI. Compound interest factors formulas

Single Payment- Compound Amount Factor	(F/P, i%, n)	$(1 + i)^n$

Single Payment- Present Worth Factor	(P/F, i%, n)	$\dfrac{1}{(1+i)^n}$
Sinking Fund Factor	(A/F, i%, n)	$\dfrac{i}{(1+i)^n-1}$
Capital Recovery Factor	(A/P, i%, n)	$\dfrac{i(1+i)^n}{(1+i)^n-1}$
Uniform Series- Compound Amount Factor	(F/A, i%, n)	$\dfrac{(1+i)^n-1}{i}$
Uniform Series-Present Worth Factor	(P/A, i%, n)	$\dfrac{(1+i)^n-1}{i(1+i)^n}$

VII. Sample Problems

Problems:

1. A man borrowed P2,000.00 from a bank and promised to pay the amount for one year. He received only the amount f P 1,920 after the bank, collected an advance interest of P80.00

a). What is the rate of interest given and collected in advance.?

b). What is the rate of discount given by the bank?

c). What is the difference between the rate of interest and the rate of discount.

Solution:

a). Rate of interest:

$$\text{Rate of Interest} = \frac{\text{Interest}}{\text{Principal}}$$

$$\text{Rate of Interest} = \frac{80}{1920}$$

$i = 0.0417$ say 4.17%

b). Rate of discount:

$$\text{Rate of discount} = \frac{\text{Interest}}{\text{Principal}}$$

$$\text{Rate of discount} = \frac{80}{2000} \times 100 = 4\%$$

c). Difference= Rate of Interest – Rate of discount

$$= 4.17 - 4.0 = 0.17\%$$

2. A P1,000 loan was made at 10% simple annual interest.

   a). Which of the following gives the time in years for the amount of the loan and interest be equal to P1700.

   b). Which of the following gives the interest charged after 5 years

   c). Which of the following gives the amount that the borrower would be willing to pay after 4 years.

Solution:

a). Time when the amount becomes P1,700

$$F = P + P r t$$

$$1700 = 1000 + 1000 \, (0.10) \, t$$

$$t = 7 \text{ years}$$

b). Interest after 5 years

$$I = P r t$$

$$I = 1000 \, (0.10)(5)$$

$$I = P500$$

c). Amount to be paid after 4 years

$$F = P + P r t$$

$$F = 1000 + 1000 \, (0.10)(4)$$

$$F = 1400$$

VIII. Other Nomenclature

Find Present Value (P) - Simple

P = M / 1 + RT

Principal = Maturity Value / 1 + Rate x Time in Years

Face Value: amount shown on the face of a note

Find Interest (I) - Simple

I = PRT

Interest = Principal **Rate** Time in Years

Find Maturity Value (M) - Simple

M = P (1 + RT)

Maturity Value = Principal (1 + Rate x Time in Years)

Maturity Value: Total amount, principal and interest that must be repaid when a loan is paid off

Find Maturity Value / Face Value (M) - Discount

M = P / (1 - DT)

Maturity / Face Value = Proceeds / (1 - Discount Rate x Time in Years

Maturity Value: Total amount, principal and interest that must be repaid when a loan is paid off

Find Proceeds (P) - Discount

P = M – B

Proceeds = Maturity Value – Discount

Proceeds: Borrowed amount received after subtracting the discount from the face value of a note

hapter Three

IX. Assessment

This Interest and Discount is arrays of chapter summary templates. To the students, professionals, bankers, lenders and investors: Should something hampers our decision on basic Interest- Discount mathematical approaches; let us just visit our undertakings in this chapter. On interest formula, simple discount, comparative formula presentation, compound formula presentation and sample problems.

*"The reading of all good books is like conversation with the finest men of past centuries." - **Descartes***

*According to **Bill Gates** - It's fine to celebrate success but it is more important to heed the lessons of failure. I choose a lazy person to do a hard job, because a lazy person will fine an easy way to do it".*

So that mathematics always come an easy connectivity to other sciences. Math goal setting is a powerful process for personal and business planning. The process of setting goals helps you choose where you want to go in life and in your new business venture. By knowing precisely what you want to achieve, you know where you will have to concentrate your efforts. You'll also quickly spot the distractions that would otherwise lure you from your course.

Math is a very useful tool and technique that helps you learn more effectively, improves the way that you record information, and supports and enhances creative problem solving.

By using mathematics to analyze a problem, you can quickly identify and understand the structure of a subject. You can see the way that pieces of information fit together, as well as recording the raw facts contained in normal situations.

More than this, training of you mind through mathematics help you remember information, as they hold it in a format that your mind finds easy to recall and quick to review.

THE ECONOMIES OF SCALE

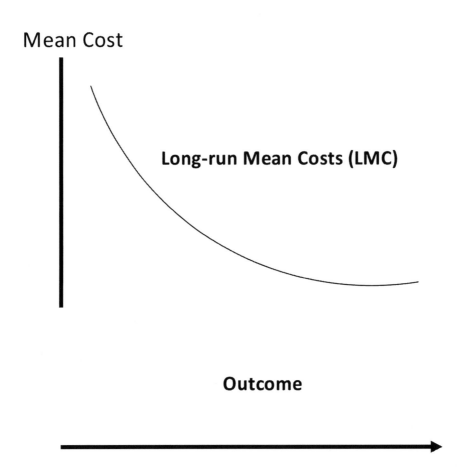

Mean Cost

Long-run Mean Costs (LMC)

Outcome

Economies of Scale or Increasing returns to scale is equal to Mean Costs over the Outcome:

LMC

Economies of Scale = —————

Outcome

The Principle – Economies of scale are increasing returns which are achieved when the mean costs (cost divided by outcome) **decrease** as output (the volume of production) **rises.** This is a proportionate saving in costs gained by an increased level of production, as a company grows and production units increase, a company will have a better chance to decrease its costs.

CHAPTER FOUR

TIME VALUE MONEY

*"The best way to predict the future is to create it. Management is doing things right; leadership is doing the right things". – **Peter Drucker***

I. OBJECTIVE, PURPOSE AND APPROACH

➤ *To establish a working knowledge conducive to solving business problems*

➤ *To learn what is it all about business math and its applicability to real estate practice*

➤ *To allow the opportunity to identify one from the other*

➤ *To introduce analytical skills necessary to be successful the intricacies towards decision making*

After this chapter, you will have learned:

❖ Review and learned the keystone concepts, theories and practices concerning basic time value of money, and through governing fund management

❖ Understand the external and intrinsic factors that impact of theorem and real business practice.

❖ Acquire the requisite fundamental and technical tools for investment decision-making

❖ Think critically about how theory and practice interact in the real the real estate industry

❖ Apply your learned competencies in creating a fund, designing its strategy defend your investment outcome

❖ Gain knowledge and skill that adds value to your financial or investments.

❖ How to prepare the Compounding and Discounting of business for an interesting and understanding problems solving as a tool for a thorough analysis;

❖ How to tell your business clients on the different time value of money for decision making;

❖ How to knowledgeably present, persuasively convince, and finally become friend with the client on the service or product you bring across the coffee table.

Industry stakeholders

In any economic conditions of real estate, market is dominated by supply and demand analysis between buyer and seller. The supply and demand cycle whether by design or by natural evolution is how population grows with its income stream

II. Compound Interest

Compound interest. Whenever at stipulated intervals during the term of an investment, the interest due is added to the principal and thereafter earns interest, the sum which represents the increase in the original principal at the end of the term is called compound interest.

Compound amount. It is the total amount due which is the sum of the original principal and the compound interest.

Conversion period. It is the time between successive conversions of interest into principal. Conversion periods are monthly (m=12), quarterly (m=4), semi-annually (m=2), and annually (m=1).

III. Future Value vs Present Value formula (1)

Compound Interest Formula:

$$FV = PV \ (1 + i)^n$$

Where:

FV = Future value (compound amount)

PV = Present value (original principal)

i = Interest rate per conversion period

j = Divided by the conversion period (m)

n = Total conversion periods per year (m) multiplied by the time (t)

Example 1 - Find the future value or the compounded amount and its interest if P15,000 is invested at 10% compounded quarterly for 5 years.

Solution : Interest rate per conversion period

$$i = j \ / \ m = 10\% \ / \ 4 = 2.5\%$$

total number of conversion periods

$n = mt = 4 (5) = 20$

Compound Amount formula

$FV = PV (1 + i)^n$

$= P15,000 (1 + .025)^{20}$

$= 1 + .025)^{20} = 1.638616$

$= P15,000 (1.638616)$

$= P24,579.24$

Compound Interest

Interest = Future Value- Present Value

I = FV - PV

$= P24,579.24 – P15,000$

$= P9,579.24$

Example 2 - Accumulate P5,000 at 12% compounded semi-annually for 4 years and 10 months.

Solution: To accumulate a principal PV for n conversion periods means to find the compound amount FV.

Interest rate per conversion period

$i = 12 / 2 = 6\%$ semi-annually

Total number of conversion periods

$n = (2)(4\ 10/12) = (9\ 2/3)$

Since n is not an integer, the compound amount FV can be solved by approximate accumulation as shown here:

a). Accumulated PV for the last whole interest period contained in the given time, to obtain an amount FV_1 on that date, use $\mathbf{FV = PV\ (1 + i)^n}$

b). Accumulate F_1 for the remaining time at simple interest at the given nominal rate, use $I = FV_1\ r\ t$

c). Add FV_1 and I to get the value of the approximate compound amount FV.

Applying the three steps to the given problem:

$n = 9$ whole interest periods

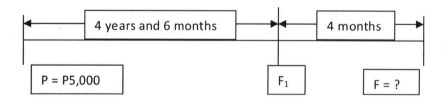

a). $F_1 = P5,000 (1 + 6\%)^9$

       $= (1 + .06)^9 = 1.68948$

       $= P5,000 (1.68948)$

       $= P8,447.40$

b). $I = (8,447.40) (.12) (4/12)$

      $= P337.90$

c). $F = P8,447.40 + P337.90$

      $= P8785.30$

Note : The theoretical amount as a tool for your double checking your problem solving ability.

$FV = PV (1 + i)^n$

$F = P5,000 (1 + 6\%)^{9\ 2/3}$

$(1 + 06)^{9\ 2/3} = 1.7564$

   $= P5,000 (1.7564)$

   $= P8,781.998$

Present Value of F and compound Discount - To discount an amount FV for n conversion periods means to find its present value PV on a day which n periods before FV is due. From **FV = PV $(1 + i)^n$** the present value PV is obtained by :

Formula Table Derivation

PERIOD	PRESENT	INTEREST	TOTAL AMOUNT
1	P	Pi	$P + Pi = P(1 + i)$
2	$(1 + i)$	$P(1 + i)i$	$P(1 + i)(1 + i) = P(1 +)^2$
3	$(1 + i)^2$	$P(1 + i)^2 i$	$P(1 + i)^2(1 + i) = P(1 +)^3$
n			$(1 + i)^n$

PV = FV $(1 + i)^{-n}$ .Get values of the discount factor $(1 + i)^{-n}$

D = F - P

Example 3 - Buying a car worth P800,000 as a gift to his son when he graduates from college 5 years from now, how much should the parents save money today as an investment at 10% compounded semi-annually.

Solution:

P = F $(+ i)^{-n}$

= P800,000 $(1 + 5\%)^{-10}$

= **P491,130.60**

Example 4 - If money is worth 7 1/2 % compounded monthly, find the discount if P500,000 is discounted for 25 years.

Solution : Interest rate per conversion period

i = 7 1/2 / 12 = 5/8%

Total conversion periods

n = (12) (25) = 300

PV = FV (1 + i)$^{-n}$

= 500,000(1.00625)$^{-300}$

=P77,126.21

Note : This is the same amount that can be obtained using a formula base computation.

Example 4 (1)- A firm borrows P5,000 for 8 years. How much must it repay in a lump sum at the end of the 8th year?

SOLUTIONS

a). Cash Flow Diagram : Compound Interest Future Value

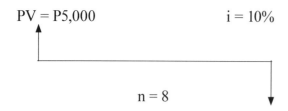

PV = P5,000   i = 10%

n = 8

FV = ?

b). FORMULA BASE SOLUTION:

$FV = PV (1 + i)^n$

$(1 + i)^{xy} 8 = 1.1^8 = 2.1436$

$= P5,000 (2.1436)$

$FV = P10,718$

c). Calculator Base (EL-733A) Solution

Fin Mode   2ndF   CA   2ndF   TAB 2

8 [n]   10 [i]   5,000 [PV]   COMP[FV]

FV = P10,718

d). MS EXCEL 2007 Base Solution

= FV (B3,B2,0,-B1)

FV = P10,717

B5		f_x =FV(B2,B3,0,B1)		
	A	B	C	D
1	Present Value **PV**	5000		
2	Interest Rate **i**	0.1		
3	Period **n**	8		
4	Payment **PMT**			
5	Future Value **FV**	($10,717.94)	ANSWER	
6				

FV = P10,717.94

B5		f_x =FV(B2,B3,0,-B1)		
	A	B	C	D
1	Present Value **PV**	5000		
2	Interest Rate **i**	0.1		
3	Period **n**	8		
4	Payment **PMT**			
5	Future Value **FV**	$10,717.94		
6				

Note: On the above example; both solution are correct but why the other is color red? The difference is on the input of the negative sign only.

IV. Present Value vs Future Value formula (2)

Example 4 (2) - A firm desires to have P7,000 six years from now. What amount should be deposited now to provide for it? At 10% interest.

Solutions:

a). **Cash Flow Diagram**

Discounting factors

Discounted Cash Flow (DCF)

$$i = 10\% \qquad n = 6$$

FV = P 7,000

PV = ?

b). FORMULA BASE SOLUTION

PV=FV(1+i)$^{-n}$

$(1 + i)^6 = 1/x$

= 0.5645

= P 7,000 (0.5645)

PV = **P 3,951.50**

c). Calculator Base (EL-733A) Solution

Fin Mode   2ndF   CA   2ndF   TAB 2

6 [n]   10 [i]   7,000 [FV]   COMP[PV]

PV = P3,951.50

d). MS EXCEL 2007 Base Solution

= PV (D3,D2,0,D4)

PV = P3,951.32

	B1		f_x	=PV(B2,B3,0,B5)	
	A	B	C	D
1	Present Value **PV**	($3,951.32)	←	
2	Interest Rate **i**	0.1		
3	Period **n**	6		
4	Payment **PMT**			
5	Future Value **FV**	$7,000.00		
6				

Example 4 (3) - If 3 annual deposits of P3,000 each are placed in an account, how much money has accumulated after the last deposit ?

Solutions:

a). Cash Flow Diagram

Compound amount of one per period

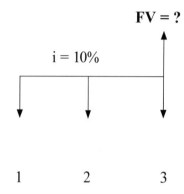

PMT = P3,000 Future of one per period

V. Future Value vs Annuity (3)

$$FV = PMT \ [(1 + i)^n - 1]/i)$$

b). $1.1^3 - 1 = 0.3310/i$

$$= 3.31$$

$$= P3{,}000 \ (3.31)$$

FV   = **P9,930**

B5		f_x	=FV(B2,B3,B4,0)	
	A	B	C	D
1	Present Value **PV**			
2	Interest Rate **i**	0.1		
3	Period **n**	3		
4	Payment **PMT**	3000		
5	Future Value **FV**	($9,930.00)	←	
6				

Example 5 (4) - What uniform yearly amount should be deposited annually in order to have P15,000 at the time of the 5th annual deposit?

Solutions

Cash Flow Diagram

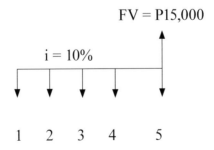

FV = P15,000

i = 10%

1   2   3   4   5

PMT = ?

VI. Annuity vs Future Value formula (4)

$$PMT = FV[i/(1+i)^n - 1]$$

$$= i/(1+.10)^5 - 1$$

$$= 0.1638$$

$$= P15,000 (0.1638)$$

$$PMT = P2,457$$

	A	B	C	D
		B4	f_x =PMT(B2,B3,0,B5)	
1	Present Value **PV**			
2	Interest Rate **i**	0.1		
3	Period **n**	5		
4	Payment **PMT**	($2,456.96)	←	
5	Future Value **FV**	$15,000.00		
6				

Example 6 (5) - How much should be deposited in a fund now to provide for 9 end-of-year withdrawals of P300 each

Cash Flow Diagram

Present value of an annuity

PMT   = P300

i = 10%

n = 9

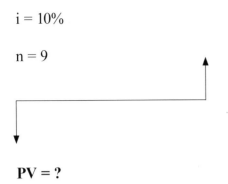

PV = ?

FORMULA BASE SOLUTION

VII. Present Value vs Annuity formula (5)

$$PV = PMT \, [(1-(1 + i)^{-n}/i$$

$1.1^9 = 1/X = 0.4241$

PV = P300 (5.7590)

PV = P1,727.7

	B1	f_x	=PV(B2,B3,B4,0)	
	A	B	C	D
1	Present Value **PV**	($1,727.71)	⟵	
2	Interest Rate **i**	0.1		
3	Period **n**	9		
4	Payment **PMT**	$300.00		
5	Future Value **FV**			
6				

Example 7 (6) - What is the size of 10 equal annual payments (amortization) to repay a loan of P3,000?

Cash Flow Diagram

PV = P 1,000   i = 10%

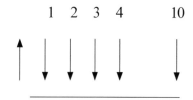

PMT = ?

FORMULA BASE SOLUTION

VIII. Annuity vs Present Value formula (6)

PMT = PV[i /1–(1 + i)$^{-n}$]

1.1^{10} = 1/x = .3855

(1-.3855) = i/.6145

= 0.1627

PMT = P3,000 (0.1627)

PMT = P488.10

	A	B	C	D
1	Present Value **PV**	$3,000.00		
2	Interest Rate **i**	0.1		
3	Period **n**	10		
4	Payment **PMT**	($488.24)		
5	Future Value **FV**			
6				

B4 f_x =PMT(B2,B3,B1,)

PMT =-162.75

EXCEL 2007 BASE SOLUTION = PMT(B3,B2,B1,0)

PV   1,000

N   10

I   10%

Pmt   **162.75**

Example 8 (7) - Problem In how many years is required for P2,000 to increase by P3,000 if interest at 12% compounded semi-annually?

$$FV = PV (1+i)^n$$

0 1 2 3   n?

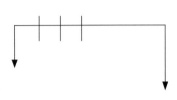

2000   2,000+3,000

$$2000 + 3000 = 2000 (1+0.12/2)^{2n}$$

$$2.5 = (1.06)^{2n}$$

Take log on both sides:

Log $2.5 = \log(1.06)^{2n}$

$\log 2.5 = 2n\log 1.06$

$\log 2.5/\log 1.06 = 2n$

n = 7.86

The money will increase by P3,000 in 7.86 years

Example 10 1.2 - Solving for the Number of Periods

Sometimes you know how much money you have now, and how much you need to have at an undetermined future time period. If you know the interest rate, then you can solve for the amount of time that it will take for the present value to grow to the future value by solving for n.

Suppose that you have $1,250 today and you would like to know how long it will take you double your money to $2,500.

Assume that you can earn 9% per year on your investment.

This is the classic type of problem that we can quickly approximate using the Rule of 72. However, we can easily find the exact answer using the NPer function. As the name suggests, this function is designed to solve for the number of periods and is defined as:

NPer(rate, pmt, pv, *fv, type***)**

Create a new worksheet and enter the data shown below:

	A	B	C	D	E
1	Present Value	1,250			
2	Future Value	2,500			
3	Annual Rate	9%			
4					
5	Number of Periods	8.04 ◄———		=NPER(B3,0,-B1,B2)

B6	▼	f_x =NPER(B3,0,B1,B4)		
▲	A	B	C	D	E
1	Present Value PV	-1250			
2	Period n				
3	Interest Rate i	9%			
4	Future Value FV	2500			
5	Payment PMT				
6		8.043232			

Select B5 and type: =NPER(B3,0,-B1,B2). You can see that it will take 8.04 years to double your money. One important thing to note is that you absolutely must enter your according to the cash flow sign convention.

If you don't make either the PV or FV a negative number (and the other one positive), then you will get a #NUM error instead of the answer. That is because, if both numbers are positive, Excel thinks that you are getting a benefit without making any investment.

If you get this error, just fix the problem by changing the sign of either PV or FV. In this problem it doesn't really matter which one is negative. The key is that they must have opposite signs.

Note that in this problem we wanted to know how long it will take to double your money at 9%. The exact numbers for the PV and FV don't matter as long as the FV is exactly twice the PV. You can prove this by changing the PV to 1 and the FV to 2. You will get exactly the same answer.

Example (8) i - An amount of P1,000 becomes P1,608.44 after 4 years compounded bimonthly. Find the nominal interest

$$F=P(1+i)^n \qquad i= ?$$

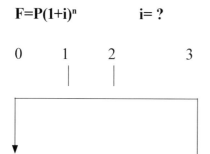

1,000 - - - - - - - - - - - - - - - 1,608.44

$$1,608.44^{1/24} = 1,000 (1+i)^{4(6)}$$

$$1.02=1+i$$

$$I+0.02$$

$$1.60844^{24} [1/x] = 1.02$$

But: $i=NR/m$

$$0.02=NR/6$$

Therefore nominal rate is 12%

Example 11 - A loan for P50,000 to be paid in 3 years at the amount of P65,000. What is the effective rate of money?

$$FV=PV(1+i)^n$$

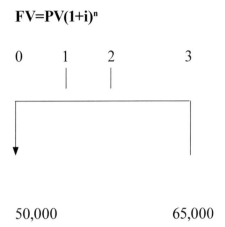

50,000   65,000

$$65,000 = 50,000 (1+i)^3$$

$$1.3=(1+i)^3 \quad 1.3^{1/3} = 1.0914$$

$$1.0914=1+i$$

$$i=9.14\%$$

IX. Doubling Time

Example 12 - How long will it take money to double itself if invested at 5% compounded annually?

$$FV = PV (1+i)^n$$

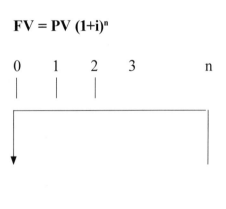

P   F=2P

To double the money,   F=2P

$2P=P(1+i)^n$

$2=(1+0.05)^n$

Take log on both sides

$Log2=nlog1.05$

N=14.2 years

When will an amount be tripled with an interest of 11.56%

$FV = PV (1+i)^n$

0   1   2   3   **n = ?**

P   F=3P

$3P=P(1+0.1156)^n$

$3=(1.1156)^n$

$n=log3/log1.1156$

n=10.04 years

The amount will triple in 10 years

Example: How many years will a PV of P5,250 doubles to FV of P10,500 on a 12% interest

B3		▼	f_x =NPER(B2,0,-B1,B5)		
◢	A	B	C	D	
1	Present Value **PV**	$5,250.00			
2	Interest Rate **i**	0.12			
3	Period **n**	6.116255374	←		
4	Payment **PMT**				
5	Future Value **FV**	$10,500.00			
6					

Example: Find the Net Present Value (NPV) on a interest rate of 10%, with an initial investment of $100,000 with a five years period.

Interest Rate   0.1

Initial Investment   -100,000

Period		Total	Yearly PV
1	25,000	$22,727.27	
2	25,000	$43,388.43	$20,661.16
3	25,000	$62,171.30	$18,782.87
4	25,000	$79,246.64	$17,075.34

5	25,000	$94,769.67	$15,523.03
6	25,000	**$108,881.52**	$14,111.85
	$8,881.52		**$108,881.52**

NPV = $8,881.52

The same example in an Excel formulae: NPV(rate,net_inflow)+initial_investment PV(rate,year_number,yearly_net_inflow)

		10% rate		
			Total	Yearly PV
		-100000		
	1	25000	₪ -22,727.27	
	2	25000	₪ -43,388.43	₪ -20,661.16
	3	25000	₪ -62,171.30	₪ -18,782.87
	4	25000	₪ -79,246.64	₪ -17,075.34
	5	25000	₪ -94,769.67	₪ -15,523.03
	6	25000	₪ -108,881.52	₪ -14,111.85
		₪ 8,881.52	**PV(rate,A10,B10)**	
		NPV(rate,net_inflow)+initial_investment		

Then, double check with your excel generated computation

There are at least three approaches to growth rate:

Formula:

- Exponential Growth Rate

- Geometrical Growth Rate

- Linear Growth Rate

I deeply pondered on the theory of **Robert Malthus:**

In *Essay on the Principle of Population,* Malthus proposes the principle that human populations grow exponentially (i.e., doubling with each cycle) while food production grows at an arithmetic rate (i.e. by the repeated addition of a uniform increment in each uniform interval of time). Thus, while food output was likely to increase in a series of twenty-five year intervals in the arithmetic progression 1, 2, 3, 4, 5, 6, 7, 8, 9, and so on, population was capable of increasing in the geometric progression 1, 2, 4, 8, 16, 32, 64, 128, 256, and so forth. This scenario of arithmetic food growth with simultaneous geometric human population growth predicted a future when humans would have no resources to survive on. To avoid such a catastrophe, Malthus urged controls on population growth. http://cgge.aag.org/PopulationandNaturalResources1e/CF_PopNatRes_Jan10/CF_PopNatRes_Jan108.html

This brings us to a three very important subjects in our lives we have to address now and ever:

- Food scarcity

- Population Intensity

- Environmental Degradation

Example: The population of a city in 2017 is 211,879. The population then, in 2012 registered at 184,970.

What is its growth by:

a). Linear Growth Rate

b). Geometrical Growth Rate

c). Exponential Growth Rate

a). Linear Growth Rate

$$LGR = \frac{Pn - Po}{Po} \, / \, time \ (t)$$

Given: Population 2017 (Pn) – 211,879

Population 2012 (Po) – 184,970

$$LGR = (Pn-Po/Po) \, / \, Time \ x \ 100$$

a). **LGR** =

$$\frac{211{,}879 - 184{,}970}{184.970} \ / \ 5 = 2.90\%$$

b). **Geometric Growth Rate**

$$R = [\text{antilog} \log P_n/P_o \ /t] - 1$$

$$GGR = antilog \ \frac{\log P_n}{P_o} \ [/t] - 1$$

$$= 211{,}879 \ / \ 184{,}970 = 1.0526 = (\log \ / \ 5) - 1 = 2.75\%$$

c). **Exponential Growth Rate**

$$R = [\ln \frac{P_n}{P_o} \ / \ time \ ] \times 100$$

$$EGR = [\ln \frac{P_n}{P_o} \ /t] \times 100$$

= ln 211,879/184,970

= 0.13582170772 / 5

= **2.72%**

Therefore: This divergent result by different growth rate problem solving characterization gives us a view: By

Linear Growth Rate has the   highest percentage – 2.90

Geometrical Growth Rate is in the   middle percentage – 2.75

Exponential growth Rate comes the   lowest percentage – 2.72

This is a good way of double checking our computation

hapter Four

X. Assessment

This Compound - Discount chapter is with an arrays of chapter summary templates. To the students, professionals, bankers, lenders and investors: Should something hampers our decision on basic Compound Discount mathematical approaches; let us just visit our undertakings in this chapter. On compound interest formula,

> ➢ Future Value vs Present Value Formula

> ➢ Present Value vs Future Value Formula

> ➢ Future Value vs Annuity (PMT) Formula

> ➢ Annuity (PMT) vs Future Value Formula

> ➢ Present Value vs Annuity (PMT) Formula

> ➢ Annuity (PMT) vs Present Value Formula

> ➢ Doubling Time Problems

   a). Linear

   b). Geometrical

   c). Exponential

Again, mathematics always come an easy connectivity to other sciences. Math goal setting is a powerful process for personal and business planning. The process of setting goals helps you choose where you want to go in life and in your new business venture. By knowing precisely what you want to achieve, you know where you will have to concentrate your efforts. You'll also quickly spot the distractions that would otherwise lure you from your course.

Math is a very useful tool and technique that helps you learn more effectively, improves the way that you record information, and supports and enhances creative problem solving.

By using mathematics to analyze a problem, you can quickly identify and understand the structure of a subject. You can see the way that pieces of information fit together, as well as recording the raw facts contained in normal situations.

More than this, training of you mind through mathematics help you remember information, as they hold it in a format that your mind finds easy to recall and quick to review.

Again, our approach to TIME VALUE MONEY is through

a). Diagramming – Cash Flow

b). Basic Formula

c). Calculator

d). MS Excel

$$FV = PV(1+i)^n$$
$$FV = PMT[(1+i)^n - 1]/i)$$

$$PV = FV(1+i)^{-n}$$
$$PV = PMT[(1-(1+i)^{-n}]/i$$

$$PMT = FV[\ i/(1+i)^n - 1]$$
$$PMT = PV[\ i/1-(1+i)^{-n}]$$

TIME VALUE MONEY

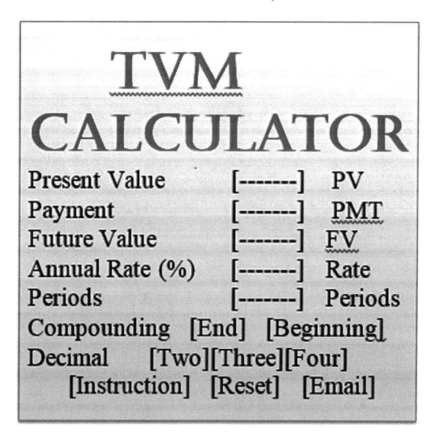

The above calculator format is a specialized snippet program on **Time Value Money** (TVM), which is a very handy tool in computing, analyzing data, and ultimately business enterprise decision making.

Time value of money is a yardstick for appraising capital expenditure in general and Net Present Value in particular for project based enterprise. It assists on an informed lease/ buy decision making analysis whether to purchase equipment or invest or lease those same funds at current forecast interest rates.

The *time value of money* is a core concept and principle of finance. "A bird in hand is better two in the bush", which means that *money* available at the present *time* is worth more than the same amount in the future. This is based on the potential earning capacity. This study helps you realize about the power of money, other than spending and buying things. The time value of money is the cost of money and is measured by the interest due over time and the loan service period.

VON THUNEN THEORY OF LAND LOCATION

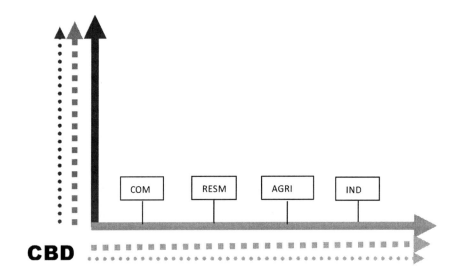

Land Uses – The farther distance you go from the **Central Business District**, the lesser the land value becomes but considering the advantages and disadvantages, the prudence and judicial planning comes by the right zoning implementation of the LGU. The land value in the center. is the most expensive.

The ***Central Business District or CBD*** - the focal point of a city with high/multi-storey buildings.

a). location of the most expensive land values.

b). Densely populated and road network.

c). limited open spaces.

HAPTER FIVE

REAL ESTATE APPRAISAL

*"No society can surely be flourishing and happy, of which the far greater part of the members are poor and miserable". - **Adam Smith** and **Socrates** said – "He is richest who is content with the least, for content is the wealth of nature."*

I. OBJECTIVE, PURPOSE AND APPROACH

➤ *To know and establish a working knowledge about real estate appraisal.*

➤ *To learn and apply what is it all about business math*

➤ *To allow the opportunity to identify between valuation and appraisal*

➢ *To introduce analytical skills necessary to be successful on the nuances and intricacies towards decision making*

After this chapter, you will have learned:

❖ The keystone concepts, theories and practices concerning basic time value of money, and through governing fund management

❖ Understood the external and intrinsic factors that impact of theorem and real business practice.

❖ Acquired the requisite fundamental and technical tools for investment decision-making

❖ Thought critically about how theory and practice interact in the real the real estate industry

❖ Have learned competencies in creating a fund, designing its strategy defend your investment outcome

❖ Gained knowledge and skill that adds value to your financial or investments.

II. PRC-PRBRES subjects guidelines

These are the subjects prescribed by PRC-PRBRES as a guide for tertiary courses. Most of the colleges and universities take a long route to attract students to the real estate service industry practice, notwithstanding the burgeoning upbeat and upscale development in the Philippines.

Real Estate Courses / Subjects

BROKER	APPRAISER	CONSULTANT
1. Fundamentals of real property ownership	1. Fundamentals of real estate principles & practices	1. Fundamentals of Real Estate Consulting
2. Code of ethics and responsibilities	2. Standards & ethics	2. Standards & Ethics
3. Legal requirements for real estate service practice	3. Theories, & principles & practices	3. Consulting Tools & Techniques, which include project feasibility study and investment measurement tools
4. Real Estate brokerage practice	4. Human & physical geography	4. Real Estate finance & economics.
5. Subdivision Development	5. Methodology of appraisal approaches	5. Real Estate consulting & investment Analyses.
6. Condominium concept	6. Valuation procedures & research	6. Consulting for specific engagement, which includes consulting for commercial, industrial, recreational and resort and hotel properties, and consulting for government & corporate and financial institutions.

7. Real estate finance & economics

7. Appraisal of machinery & equipment

7. Land management system and real property laws, & any other related subjects as may be determined by the Board.

8. Basic Principles of ecology

8. Practical appraisal mathematics Appraisal report writing

8. Case studies –This is an add on (falling under other related subjects)

9. Urban & rural land use, planning development & zoning

10. Legal aspect of sale, mortgage & lease

10. Real estate finance & economics

11. Documentation & registration

11. Case studies

12. Real property laws, & any other related subjects as may be determined by the Board

12. Land management system & real property laws & any other related subjects as may be determined by the Board

Nevertheless and even so, we foresee an upsurge of interest from parents, students alike and the enthuse interest and embrace the opportunities to come in to the portal of the real estate industry. We have a tremendous backlog of housing in the entire country, as well as guided choice of subdivision sites plan and development. There is a huge gap on population density and household units, and the disparity between rural and urban living lifestyle. This is for the reason among choices on how to appreciate and appraise raw land to housing development. This is a big challenge confronting developers on profitability, livability, quality and affordability from subdivision home buyer. The most soothing added value is developer corporate social responsibility to give service to the community.

III. Appraisal Basic terms

Value - Fair market value (FMV) or market value means the same thing, it is an estimate of what market dictates of an asset or property, the seller and buyer are knowledgeable, willing, and able without compulsion to decide or undertake in an open market. This estimate may differ from an intrinsic value

Cost - The amount you paid for the product or services with the profit to it.

Price – Price is the amount paid for buying or acquiring any product or service.

Value - The amount incurred in producing and maintaining an asset

IV. Different appraisal uses:

1. **Loan Purposes** -.The loan-to-value (**LTV**) ratio is an interest of an appraisal client for submission to a potential lender as a basis for making loan decision.

2. **Asset value** – To determine the asset of an individual, family or corporation.

3. **Equity Build-up** – To develop a position in the preparation of a business expansion.

4. **Business Venture** – To capitalize for a projected enterprise

5. **Family Interest** – To know what is the value of a family asset

6. **Governmental Requirement** – Likely, for tax purposes.

7. **Sale** – As a tool for decision making for buyer and seller

8. **Divorce** – To use for separating asset of a married couple.

9. **Merger and Acquisition** – To use as capital or for sale

10. **Buy, etceteras** – This a popular need for appraisal for selling or buying decision

V. Define the Problem – *Fair Market Value* is the core and responsibility of an appraiser before engaging the services of a particular assignment. It requires a defined issue or the problems and identifying the factors related at hand. It helps create a clear understanding of what needs to be decided and can influence the choice between alternatives. Why and where would the need for appraisal.

VI. Appraisal Plan - It should be an efficient analysis on travel time to subject property location as well as accomplishment criteria to a benefit and cost effective undertakings.

1. **Location Identification** – Identify the subject property, either it is on a rural or urban area, its distance and average travel time and how long will it take before coming back to the office.

2. **Route guide** – Mostly, we have now a very efficient way of travel to subject property. Thanks to google map, GPS or other ways of navigation

3. **Schedule of Inspection** – It must be a man-hour proposition on when to go and get back.

4. **Collect data in order of use** – Identify all data necessary from the table appraisal to actual site inspection.

5. **Documents needed for appraisal**

   a. Title Photo Copies

   b. Certified Geodetic Engineer's Plan

   c. Building Floor Plan

   d. Tax Documents of Land and Building

   e. Tax Receipts

   f. Guide to the site and permission given and by whom

VII. Title Verification – A verified copy of the original document which has been signed and dated by someone who can confirm that it is the same as the original from the Registry of Deeds of the city, municipality or province.

VIII. General Data Analysis - The process of gathering data which the goal is discovering useful information, suggesting conclusions, and supporting decision-making. Data analysis has multiple facets and approaches, encompassing diverse techniques under a variety of names, in different business, science, and social science domains

1. Inspection

2. Check

3. Transform

4. Model

5. Geography Analysis

   a). Location

   b). State

   c). Region

   d). City

   e). Municipality

   f). Neighborhood

6. **Economic** - A market analysis is a quantitative and qualitative assessment of its market. It looks into the size of the market both in volume and in value, the various customer segments and real estate cycle, selling and buying patterns, the competition, and the economic environment in terms of barriers to entry and regulation.

   a). Market Analysis

   b). Financial

   c). Economic Base

d). Trends and Growth Rate

e). Supply and Demand

7. **Specific Data** – Answers to different and specific questions from the subject property for appraisal is required: is it house and lot, house alone, or lot only, and how about improvements. This is now an analysis of its surrounding environment, neighborhood, and conformity of the title to inspection observations of the title and on to the time of inspection and date of the report.

This is a thorough analysis on the following:

a). Subject Property

b). Title

c). Site

d). Physical

e). Highest and Best Use

f). Zoning

8. **Methods and Analysis** – Its is a strategy of data gathering for analysis by comparative or market data, by costing of the land or improvements in square meter, or square foot construction or engineering method

a). Comparative

b). Costs

   c). Sales

   d). Rentals

   e). Expenses

9. **Present Title** – Check whether title is not spurious, regarding encumbrances, clouds in the title, liens and other annotations and may be one of the following:

   a). clean

   b). mortgage

   c). adverse claims

   d). annotation, etcetera

10. **Preceding Title**

   a). First trace back

   b). Second trace back

   c). Correlation with present title

11. **Physical Inspection** - Documents requirements to actual site, building and improvements and other annexes inspection analysis.

a). Title and Tax Declaration

b). Building Plan

c). Location

d). Plotting

e). Cadastral Reference

f). Sketch Plan

g). Map/Tax Mapping

12. **Type of Neighborhood Analysis**

a). Population

b). Density

c). Income Level

d). Economic Base

e). Stage of Development

13. **Improvement Inspection Analysis**

a). Building Frameworks

b). Depreciation

c). Physical Obsolescence

d). Functional Defects

e). Age and Design

14. **Methods and Approach to Value**

a). Cost

b). Market Data

c). Income

d). Development

15. **Value Reconciliation**

a). Income

b). Cost

c). Market

d). Development

16. **Final Estimate of Value** – This is now where the nitty-gritty of an appraiser profession starts.

The client will question your appraisal value formation result:

a). Question on the comparable used

b). The appraisal methodology

c). The economic trend data analysis employed

d). Simply the client is not satisfied with the appraisal done.

This is now the time that persuasive negation comes into play. Appraisal is not rigid, it is flexible. In any way, without sacrificing service quality. It is the ability through extensive study and long experience that gets and put all things in order.

IX. Write the report

1. Forwarding letter

2. Certificate of value Signature

3. Narrative presentation

4. Picture Presentation

5. Sketch plan

6. Limiting Condition

7. Partial List of Clients

8. License Registration

9. Credential

10. Confidentially

X. Construction Cost

Construction Cost – There are many sources of construction data that one may source and adapt from. These answers to how much will it cost to build, coming from different standards of costing.

1. Developers

2. Building Contractors

3. Real Estate Brokers

4. Real Estate Appraisers

5. Construction Cost guidebooks.

    a). Condominium - Per square-meter or per square-foot, from market and construction / builders' cost data.

    b). **Residential** - Per square meter or per square-foot, from market and build cost.

    c). **Raw land** - Per square meter or per square foot, from mark or build cost

Market Data or Market Comparable - This is a source of information for appraisal data gathering

Physical depreciation - Depreciation is the reduction or fall in the value of an asset or physical property during the course of its working life and due to the passage of time.

XI. Types of Depreciation:

1. **Physical Depreciation** is due to the reduction of the physical ability of a property or equipment, or asset to produce results.

2. **Functional Depreciation** is due to the reduction in the demand for function that the equipment or asset was designed to render.

This type of depreciation is often called obsolescence

DEPRECIATION METHOD
REAL ESTATE

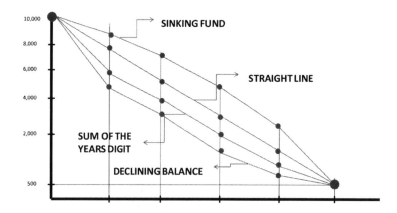

Methods of Computing Depreciation:

a). STRAIGHT LINE METHOD

In this method of computing depreciation, it is assumed that the loss in value is directly proportional to the age of the equipment or asset.

Example: Economic life is a kind of construction materials used in the building. There is a numerous choice on the right materials to use and through the detailed engineering bill of materials costing may be arrived at. Say for example the building will have an economic life of 40 years, which is fair enough. So that a hundred percent over economic life is 2.5% (100/40) on a straight line method. This bench-mark at 2.5% may go up or on the contrary goes down. It now depends on its actual use over the years. The useful life may go more than its economic life on many factors:

1. Efficient maintenance

2. Periodic upgrading

3. Kind of use

Formula:

Economic Life - Used life = Remaining Economic Life

Annual depreciation charge, d

$d = C_o - C_n$ over n

where:

C_o = first cost

C_n = cost after 'years (salvage/scrap value)

n = life of the property

Book value at the end of "m" years of using, C_m

$Cm = C_o - D_m$

where:

Dm = total depreciation after "m" years

$D_m = d\,(m)$

b). SINKING FUND METHOD

In this method of computing depreciation, it is assumed that a sinking fund is established in which funds will accumulate for replacement purposes.

Annual depreciation charge, d

$d + i)^n - 1$

where: C_o = first cost

C_n = cost after "n" years (salvage/scrap value)

n = life of the property

$Cm = C_o - D_m$

where: D_m = total depreciation after "m" years

$$D_m = d[(1 +)^m -1] / i$$

c). DECLINING BALANCE METHOD

In this method of computing depreciation, it is assumed that the annual cost of depreciation is a fixed percentage of the book value at the beginning of the year. This method is sometimes known as constant percentage method or the Matheson Formula.

Matheson Formula

$k = 1 -$ square   or $k = 1 - m$ square root C_m/C_o

The value k is the constant percentage. Hence, k must be decimal and a value less than 1. In this method, the salvage or scrap value must not be zero.

d). SUM-OF-THE YEARS' DIGIT (SYD) METHOD

First year: $d1 = [(C_o - C_n) n] / $ Summation of years

Second year $d2 = [(C_o - C_n)] n-1 / $ Summation of years

Third year $d3 = [(C_o - C_n) n]-2 / $ Summation of years and

so on

Book value at the end of "m" years of using, Cm

$Cm = C_o - (d1 + d2 + \ldots + dm)$

Summation of years $= n(n + 1)/2$

XII. Comparison of depreciation Methods

For comparison between the different methods of depreciations, let us consider the following data;

First cost	$C_0 = P20,000$
Salvage value	$C_n = P5,000$
Life of property	$n = 5$ years

a). **Using straight line method:** A machine costs P20,000 with a salvage value of P5000 with the machine economic life-span of five years.

$$d \quad = C_0 - C_n / n$$

$$d \quad = 20,000 - 5000 / 5$$

$$d \quad = 15,000 / 5 = 3000$$

Salvage Value = P5000 (in accounting book value assigned depreciation). In real estate appraisal practice is by actual physical inspection done or as dictated by the market

Tabulation

Period	Depreciation	Book value
0		20,000

1	3,000	17,000
2	3,000	14,000
3	3,000	11,000
4	3,000	8,000
5	3,000	5,000

b). Using sinking fund method:

Assume 10% interest rate

Co = 20,000

Cn = 5,000

$D = (C_o - C_n) \, i / (1 + I)^n - 1$

$d = (20,000 - 5,000)(.10) / (1 + .10)^5 - 1$

$= (1.1)^5 - 1 = 0.611$

$d = 1,500 / 0.61051 = 2,456.96$

$D_1 = \quad d = 2,456.96$

$D_2 = d[(1 + i)^2 - 1] / i$

$= 2,456.96[(1 + 0.1)^2 - 1]/i$

$(1.1)^2 - 1 = 0.210$

$= 5,159.62$

$D_3 = d[(1 + i)^3 - 1] / i$

$= 2{,}456.96[(1 + 0.1)^3 - 1] / i$

$(1.1)^3 - 1 = 0.331$

$= 8{,}132.55$

$D_4 = d[(1 + i)^4 - 1] / i$

$= 2456.9622[(1 + 0.1)^4 - 1] / i$

$(1.1)4 - 1 = 0.4641$

$= 11{,}402.76$

$D_5 = d[(1 + i)^5 - 1] / i$

$= 2456.96[(1 + 0.1)^5 - 1] / i$

$(1.1)5 - 1 = 61051$

$= 15{,}000$

Tabulation of book value

Period	Depreciation	Book value
0		20,000
1	2456.96	17,540.38

2	5159.62	14,840.38
3	8132.55	11,867.45
4	11,402.76	8,597.24
5	15,000	5,000.00

c). **Using declining balance method** in this method of computing depreciation, it is assumed that the annual cost of depreciation is a fixed percentage of the book value at the beginning of the year. This method is sometimes known as constant percentage method or the Matheson formula.

d). **Using SYD method**

Summation of year = (n) (n+1) over 2

Summation of year = (5) (5 +1) over 2 = 15

$d1 = (C_o - C_n)$ n over Summation of year

= 20,000 -5000) 5/15

= 5000

$D2 = (C_o - C_n)$ n over Summation of year

=20,000 -5000) 4/15

= 4,000

D3 = $(C_o - C_n)$ n over Summation of year

=20,000 -5000) 3/15

= 3,000

D4 = $(C_o - C_n)$ n over Summation of year

= 20,000 -5000) 2/15

= 2,000

D5 = $(C_o - C_n)$ n over Summation of year

= 20,000 -5000) 1/15

= 1000

Tabulation

Period	Depreciation	Book value
0		20,000
1	5,000	15,000
2	4,000	11,000
3	3,000	8,000
4	2,000	6,000
5	1,000	5,000

The diagram shows that the declining balance method has the largest annual depreciation charge and the sinking fund method has the smallest annual depreciation charges.

Again, there are four different depreciation methods:

1. **Straight Line Depreciation** –The loss in value is directly proportional to the age of the equipment or asset. The simplest and most commonly used method, straight-line depreciation is calculated by taking the purchase or acquisition price of an asset, subtracting the salvage value (value at which it can be sold once the company no longer needs it) and dividing by the total productive years for which the asset can reasonably be expected to benefit the company (or its useful life).

2. **Declining Balance** – the annual cost of depreciation is a fixed percentage of the book value at the beginning of the year. This method is sometimes known as constant percentage method or the Matheson formula

3. **Double Declining Balance** The DDB method simply doubles the straight-line depreciation amount that is taken in the first year, and then that same percentage is applied to the un-depreciated amount in subsequent years.

   DDB In year i = (2 / n) * (total acquisition cost - accumulated depreciation)

   n = number of years

Example

A P4 million, worth of equipment purchased that will have an estimated useful life of five years. The company also estimates that in five years the company will be able to sell it for P400,000 for salvage value or scrap parts.

Year	Cost	Salvage Value	Estimated Life
0	4,000,000	400,000	5

Year	Depreciation Expense	Balance Sheet	Rate
1	400,000	3,600,000	2/5
2	1,440,000	2,160,000	2/5
3	864,000	1,296,000	2/5
4	518,400	777,600	2/5
5	377,600	400,000	2/5

The double-declining-balance method produces a very aggressive depreciation schedule. The asset cannot be depreciated beyond its salvage value. In this case, P377,600 final depreciation is less than P400,000 declared as a salvage or scrap value.

4. Sum of the years Digits -

Depreciation In Year I $= (n-i+1) / n!)$
* (total acquisition cost - salvage value)

Example: For P4 million, Company ABC purchased a machine that will have an estimated useful life of five years. The company also estimates that in five years, the company will be able to sell it for P400,000 for scrap parts.

n! = 1+2+3+4+5 = 15 n = 5

Year	Cost	Salvage Value	Estimated Life
0	4,000,000	400,000	5

Year	Depreciation Expense	Balance Sheet	Rate
1	600,000	3,600,000	5/15
2	960,000	2,640,000	4/15
3	720,000	1,920,000	3/15
4	480,000	1,440,000	2/15
5	240,000	120,000	1/15

By this example a declared P400,000 salvage value of the company is way of high in terms when you employ the Sum of the year analysis turns out only P120,000.

The sum-of-year depreciation method produces a variable depreciation expense. At the end of the useful life of the asset, its accumulated depreciation is equal to the accumulated depreciation under the straight-line depreciation.

XIII. Depletion

Depletion cost is the reduction of the value of certain natural resources such as mines, oil, timber, quarries, etc., due to the gradual extraction of its contents.

Methods of Computing Depletion Charge for a year:

a). **Unit or Factor Method**

This method is dependent on the initial cost of the property and the number of units in the property. The depletion charge during any year is calculated using the following formula:

Depletion cost during any year = initial cost of property over total units in property X (units sold during the year)

b). **Percentage or Depletion Allowance Method**

The depletion charge under this method is computed from a table of data given:

Depletion Charge = Fixed Percentage or Gross Income or

Depletion Charge = 50% of the Net Taxable Income

XIV. Problem Solving

Problem 1: A real estate broker accompanied by an appraiser-broker friend went to value a property. Information and with inspection done: Building value is P7,500,000, land capitalization is 6%, with building overall rate of 14%. It has a net operating income of P1,400,000 per annum. What is the value of this commercial property?

Value of the property?

Given:

Building Value	P7,500,000
Land Capitalization Rate	6%
Building overall rate	12%
Net Operating Income	P1,400,000

Solution:

Building = 7,500,000 x 12%	P900,000
NOI = 1,400,000-900,000	P6,600,000

$$\text{Building Value} = \frac{\text{Net Operating Income}}{\text{Capitulation Rate}}$$

Building Value = 6,600,000 / 6%	11,000,000
Property Value = Building + Land	
Property Value = 11,000000 + 7,500,000	**P18,500,000**

Problem 2: An interest buyer is motivated buying a property with the only data available. What is the possible income attributable to the building?

Given:

Land Value (from market)	P55,000,000
Net operating income	4,300,000
Remaining Economic Life of Bldg 33 years	
Interest Rate (from market)	8%

Solution

Net Operating Income	P4,300,000
Less: Return on land	
P4.3M x 8%	3.400,000

Net Income attributable to building P900,000

Problem 3: A property is to be appraised: How do you analyze, process and proceed with the appraisal?

a). Bring in all of the data required

b). Make a quotation for professional fee

c). Determine why the appraisal is needed

d). Make a physical inspection

e). Communicate the report orally

   I. a, b, c, d, e

   II. c, a, b, e, d

   III. e, a, c, e, d

   IV. c, a, b, d, e

Answer IV

c).Determine the problem why the appraisal is needed

a), Bring in all the data needed for appraisal

b), Quote for a professional fee

d), Make the physical inspection

e). Communicate the report orally

As always and first thing first, know why the appraisal report is needed. Second, what is the data available from the client. The client is the property owner or perhaps a prospective buyer, or maybe one of the interested heirs.

May be, it is a property with a court case. Put simply, the appraiser must maximize the working tools by asking questions and listening to the narrative from your client.

The appraiser's professional fee must be communicated clearly with a conformed and signed, of course, with a corresponding initial payment for **Travel Overhead Working Expenses (TOWE).** Prudence and experience tells us that what if in one form or the other, the assignment did not push through or your client expectations were not met? It will end up lost of business opportunity in terms of time, money and effort down the drain, in addition to loss of goodwill.

The appraiser's personal and physical inspection on the subject property is a must. This is maybe yes or maybe no, depending on the situation. Is this accurate an accurate statement? The basic and most important rule of appraisal is that property for appraisal is physically inspected.

hapter Five

XV. Assessment

Again, mathematics so with economics and finance as well as appraisal and business valuation always come as a prerequisite to an in-dept connectivity to other branches of disciplines and other sciences.

In business formulation and decision makings, appraisal is the main thing so powerful process for personal and business plan. The process of setting goals helps you choose where you want to go in life and in your new business venture. By knowing precisely what you want to achieve, you know where you will have to concentrate your efforts. You'll also quickly spot the distractions that would otherwise lure you from the course. The sequence of getting into the core of real estate appraisal:

- Define the problem why an engagement is required

- Different appraisal uses

- Planning the appraisal

- Documents and tools for engagement

- General data analysis

- Depreciation of building or structures

- Replacement / construction New comparables

- Value formation

HAPTER SIX

INVESTMENT TOOLS

FEASIBILITY STUDY
FREQUENTLY ASKED QUESTIONS (FAQs)
a) Legally Permissible?
b) Physically Possible?
c) Environmentally Allowable?
d) Financially Viable?
e) Technically Manageable?
f) Socially Acceptable?
g) Economically Profitable?
h) Culturally Reasonable?

You can't have a healthy society unless you have healthy companies that are making a profit, that are employing people and that are growing - **Michael Porter**

I. OBJECTIVE, PURPOSE AND APPROACH

➢ *To establish an environment conducive to growth by in-depth financial and economic analysis with thorough study.*

➤ *To allow and identify opportunities for a business consulting.*

➤ *To find opportunities and strategies for business growth.*

➤ *To analyze financial tools and alternatives for decision-making.*

After this chapter, you will have learned:

❖ The keystone concepts, theories and practices concerning basic time value of money, and through governing fund management

❖ Understood the external and intrinsic factors that impact of theorem and real business practice.

❖ Acquired the requisite fundamental and technical tools for investment decision-making

❖ Thought critically about how theory and practice interact in the real the real estate industry

❖ Have learned competencies in creating a fund, designing its strategy defend your investment outcome

II. Financial Ratios

Formula

LIQUIDITY RATIOS

$$\text{RECEIVABLES TURNOVER} = \frac{\text{ANNUAL CREDIT SALES}}{\text{ACCOUNTS RECEIVABLES}}$$

CURRENT ASSET

$$\text{CURRENT RATIO} = \frac{\text{CURRENT ASSET}}{\text{CURRENT LIABILITIES}}$$

$$\text{QUICK RATIO} = \frac{\text{CURRENT ASSETS-INVENTORY}}{\text{CURRENT LIABILITIES}}$$

$$\text{CASH RATIO} = \frac{\text{CASH + MARKETABLE SECURITIES}}{\text{CURRENT LIABILITIES}}$$

ASSET TURNOVER RATIOS

$$\text{RECEIVABLES TURNOVER} = \frac{\text{ANNUAL CREDIT SALES}}{\text{ACCOUNTS RECEIVABLES}}$$

$$\text{AVERAGE COLLECTION PERIOD} = \frac{\text{ACCOUNTS RECEIVABLES}}{\text{ANNUAL CREDIT SALES/365}}$$

$$\text{AVERAGE COLLECTION PERIOD} = \frac{365}{\text{RECEIVABLES TURNOVER}}$$

$$\text{INVENTORY TURNOVER} = \frac{\text{COST OF GOODS SOLD}}{\text{AVERAGE INVENTORY}}$$

$$\text{INVENTORY PERIOD} = \frac{\text{AVERAGE INVENTORY}}{\text{ANNUAL COST OF GOODS SOLD}/365}$$

$$\text{INVENTORY PERIOD} = \frac{365}{\text{INVENTORY TURNOVER}}$$

FINANCIAL LEVERAGE RATIOS

$$\text{DEBT RATIO} = \frac{\text{TOTAL DEBT}}{\text{TOTAL ASSETS}}$$

$$\text{DEBT-TO-EQUITY RATIO} = \frac{\text{TOTAL DEBT}}{\text{TOTAL EQUITY}}$$

$$\text{INTEREST COVERAGE} = \frac{\text{EBIT}}{\text{INTEREST CHARGES}}$$

PROFITABILITY RATIOS

$$\text{GROSS PROFIT MARGIN} = \frac{\text{SALES} - \text{COST OF GOODS SOLD}}{\text{SALES}}$$

$$RETURN\ ON\ ASSETS = \frac{NET\ INCOME}{TOTAL\ ASSETS}$$

$$RETURN\ ON\ EQUITY = \frac{NET\ INCOME}{SHAREHOLDER\ EQUITY}$$

DIVIDEND POLICY RATIOS

$$DIVIDEND\ YIELD = \frac{DIVIDENDS\ PER\ SHARE}{SHARE\ PRICE}$$

$$PAYOUT\ RATIO = \frac{DIVIDENDS\ PER\ SHARE}{EARNINGS\ PER\ SHARE}$$

III. Purpose and types of ratios: - Financial ratios quantify many aspects of a business and are an integral part of the financial statement analysis. Financial ratios are categorized according to the financial aspect of the business which the ratio measures.

Liquidity ratios - measure the availability of cash to pay debt.

Activity ratios - measure how quickly a firm converts non-cash assets to cash assets.

Debt ratios - measure the firm's ability to repay long-term debt.

Profitability ratios - measure the firm's use of its assets and control of its expenses to generate an acceptable rate of return.

Market ratios - measure investor response to owning a company's stock and also the cost of issuing stock. These are concerned with the return on investment for shareholders, and with the relationship between return and the value of an investment in company's shares.

Financial ratios allow for comparisons

- between companies
- between industries
- between different time periods for one company
- between a single company and its industry average

Ratios generally hold no meaning unless they are benchmarked against something else, like past performance or another company. Thus, the ratios of firms in different industries, which face different risks, capital requirements, and industries competition, are usually not easy to compare.

IV. Statistics

The Advantages of Statistics in Business

Let us go into the use of statistics: Mainly, median and mode, and range as simple statistical tools. The ability to find the mean, or the average, of a list of numbers, is in itself an advantage in business. Statistics is the main thing summarizing numerical data using statistical methods, enhancing understanding of the consultant's actual use as much as possible before a client,

Data Collection

Collecting data to use in statistics, or summarizing the data, is only an advantage in business if a manager uses a logical approach and collects and reports data in an ethical manner. For example, he might use statistics to determine if sales levels the company achieved for the last few products launched were even close to projected sales levels. He might decide that the least-performing product needs extra investment or perhaps the company should shift resources from that product to a new product.

Research and Development

A company also uses statistics in market research and product development, using different surveys, such as random samples of consumers, to gauge the market for a proposed product. A manager conducts surveys to determine if there is sufficient demand among target consumers. Survey results might justify spending on developing the product. A product launch decision might also include a break-even analysis, such as finding out what percentage of consumers must try a new product for it to be successful.

Example 1

On your first four math tests you earned a 85, 80, 95, and a 65.

What must you earn on your next test to have a **mean score** of at least 80?

Let's call that final test X.

$(85 + 80 + 95 + 65 + X) / 5 = 80$

$(325 + X) = 400$

$X = 400 - 325$

$X = 75$

Example 2

These are the steps to design a study on an appraisal assignment. Let us have it undergo an appraisal process, but they're out of order. What's the correct order?

a). Analyze your data

b). Make a conclusion

c). Form a hypothesis

d). Define the problem

e). Collect your data

f). Display your data

a). c, d, f, e, b, a,

b). d, c, e, a, f, b,

c). d, c, e, b a, f,

d). d, f, e, c, b, a,

The correct order is **b)** d, c, e, a, f, b.

We first (d) Define the problem,

then (c) form a hypothesis,

then e) collect data.

After a) analyzing the data

we f) display the data and

b) make our conclusions about whether the hypothesis was correct.

MEAN, MEDIAN, MODE, RANGE

Mean - The sum of the values divided by the number of values.

Median - The value that fall in the middle of the array

Mode - The value that appears most often in an array

Range - The difference between the highest and the lowest in an array.

Example 3:

Houses recently sold in a subdivision for the following prices: P1,350,000, 1,500,000, 1,600,000, 1,400,000, 1,550,000, and 1,450,000, 1,600,000

Find: a. **the Mean**

10,450,000/7 = P1,492,860

Find: b. **the Median**

Put the value in order, the center value is P1,500,000

Find: c. **the Range**

The lowest value in the array is P1,350,000 and the highest Value is P1,600,000. Therefore, **Range** is P250,000

Example 4

The values of 11 houses in an "informal settlers" area as shown:

Value per house	Number of Houses
P100,000	1
175,000	5

| 200,000 | 4 |
| 700,000 | 1 |

a). Compute the **mean** value of these houses

b). Find the **median** of these houses

c). State which represent best for the values of these houses, the mean or the median

a. Mean Value

Mean = [100,000(1)+175,000(5)+200,000(4) + 700,000(1)]/11

Mean = P225,000

b. Median of these houses in thousand of pesos

100, 175, 175, 175, 175, **175**, 200, 200, 200, 200, 700

Median Value = P175,000

c. Best values of these houses is represented by the mean value

Data Research Illustration

"Philippines: nationwide house prices rising strongly, but Metro Manila's CBD is slowing" – according to Lalaine C. Delmendo

The Philippines' residential property market has performed spectacularly, due to robust economic growth. During the year to Q1 2016, the nationwide residential real estate price index rose by 9.2% (8% inflation-adjusted), according to the Bangko Sentral ng Pilipinas (BSP), the country's central bank.

Quarter-on-quarter, the index rose 1.9% (1.9% inflation-adjusted) in Q1 2016. The residential real estate price index, published every quarter, is based on bank reports on residential real estate loans.

By property type:

1. **Condominium units** saw y-o-y price increase of 12.9% (11.6% inflation-adjusted) in Q1 2016

2. **Single detached/attached house** prices rose by 8.1% (6.9% inflation-adjusted) y-o-y in Q1 2016

3. **Duplex house** prices rose by 6.7% (5.5% inflation-adjusted) y-o-y in Q1 2016

4. **Townhouse** prices rose by 8.5% (7.3% inflation-adjusted) over the same period

5. **National Capital Region** (NCR), residential property prices surged 9.7% (8.5% inflation-adjusted) during the year to Q1 2016 while in

6. **Areas Outside the NCR** (AONCR), prices rose by 9.4% (8.2% inflation-adjusted), according to the BSP.

7. On the other hand, prices of high-end condominium units in Metro Manila's CBDs rose at a much slower pace."

V. Internal rate of return

The internal rate of return (IRR), economic rate of return (ERR) the discounted cash flow rate of return is a rate of return used in capital budgeting to measure and compare the profitability of investments and also called the effective interest rate.

Definition

In more specific terms, the IRR of an investment is the discount rate at which the net present value of costs (negative cash flows) of the investment equals the net present value of the benefits (positive cash flows) of the investment.

IRR calculations are commonly used to evaluate the desirability of investments or projects. The higher a project's IRR, the more desirable it is to undertake the project. Assuming all projects require the same amount of up-front investment, the project with the highest IRR would be considered the best and undertaken first.

VI. Net Present Value

Calculation

Given a collection of pairs (time, cash flow) involved in a project, the internal rate of return follows from the net present value as a function of the rate of return. Given the (period, cash flow) pairs (n, Cn) where n is a positive integer, the total number of periods N, and the net present value NPV, the internal rate of return is given by r in:

$$NPV = \sum_{t=1}^{T} \frac{C_t}{(1+r)^t} - C_0$$

where:
C_t = net cash inflow during the period
C_0 = initial investment
r = discount rate, and
t = number of time periods

The period is usually given in years, but the calculation may be made simpler if r is calculated using the period in which the majority of the problem is defined (e.g., using months if most of the cash flows occur at monthly intervals) and converted to a yearly period thereafter. Often, the value of cannot be found analytically. In this case, numerical methods or graphical methods must be used.

Example - If an investment may be given by the sequence of cash flows

Year (n)	Cash Flow (Cn)
0	-1,000,000
1	350,000
2	560,000
3	490,000

By Calculator

$$NPV = -1,000,000 + \frac{350,000}{(1 + 10)^1} + \frac{560,000}{(1 + 10)^2} + \frac{490,000}{(1 + 10)^3}$$

= 149,135.99

Take Note: The summation of the discounted cash flow is taking the difference from the initial investment. Substantially, the initial capital is being taken care off.

Condition is positive or > 1 Accept the investment

Let us get the NPV by EXCEL - 135,578.17

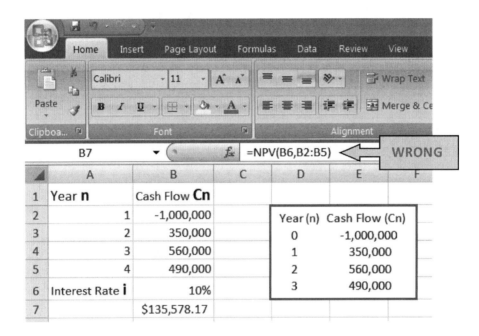

Let us get the IRR by EXCEL: Our analysis on the above excel program is something terribly wrong with the outcome of the above input. The Excel formula: = NVP(B6,B2:B5) applied here is **WRONG**:

It must be:

	A	B	C	D
		B7 ▾ f_x =NPV(B6,B3:B5)+B2		
1	Year n	Cash Flow Cn		
2	1	-1,000,000		
3	2	350,000		
4	3	560,000		
5	4	490,000		
6	Interest Rate i	0.10		
7		$149,135.99		
8	Analysis as corrected:			

$$NPV = \sum_{t=1}^{T} \frac{C_t}{(1+r)^t} - C_0$$

where:
C_t = net cash inflow during the period
C_0 = initial investment
r = discount rate, and
t = number of time periods

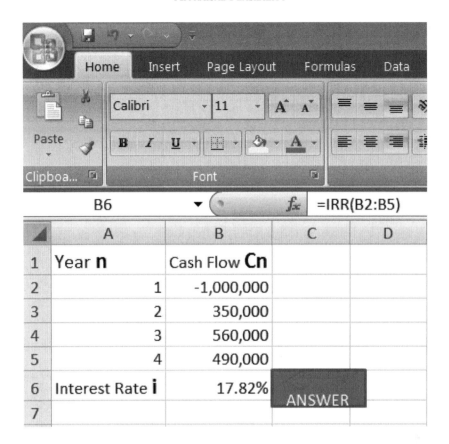

And obviously this is a good accepted project

Internal Rate of Return by Excel

Calculating Internal Rate of Return (IRR) can be tedious if you have multiple Cash Flow periods to work with. Fortunately, financial calculators and Microsoft Excel make the process amazingly simple.

Given:

YEAR	0	1	2	3
Cash Flow	-5000	1000	2000	3000

Example: Firm A wants to know whether it should buy a P5,000 worth of equipment. It projects that it will increase profits by P1,000 in Year 1, P2,000 in Year 2, and P3,000 in Year 3. Calculate the IRR of the proposed project.

Using Microsoft Excel: To find the IRR

First, type the initial cash flow into any cell on the spreadsheet. Keep in mind this initial investment has to be a negative number. Using our original example, type - **5000** into the **A1** cell of the spreadsheet. Next type **1,000** into cell A2, **2,000** into cell A3, and **3,000** into cell A4.

Finally you are ready to calculate the IRR. To instruct the Excel program to calculate IRR, type in the function command **"=IRR(A1:A4)" into the A5** cell directly under all the values. Enter key, the IRR value = 8.2%,

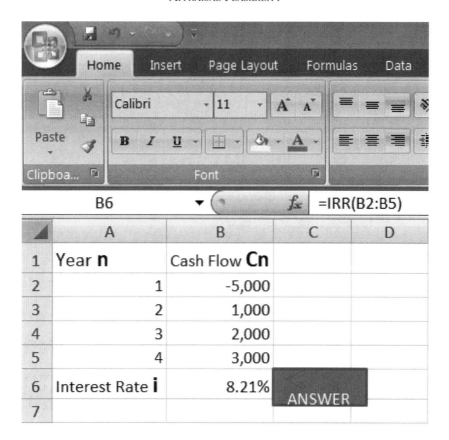

The same procedure can be followed for any data set if the cash flow values are listed one after another in a column directly under the initial investment amount. You would then put the range of cells in between the parentheses of the IRR command function.

Net present value (NPV) – The standard method for the financial appraisal of long-term projects, used for capital budgeting.

The Formula

Each cash inflow/outflow is discounted back to its PV. Then they are summed.

Therefore:

$$NPV = \sum_{t=1}^{n} \frac{C_t}{(1+r)^t} - C_0$$

Where:

t - the time of the cash flow

n - the total time of the project

r - the discount rate

C_t - the net cash flow (the amount of cash) at time t.

C_0 - the capital outlay at the beginning of the investment time ($t = 0$)

Guide of Indications

IF	IT MEANS	THEN
NPV > 0	The investment would add to the value of the firm	The project may be accepted

NPV < 0	The investment is subtracted value from the firm	The project should be rejected
NPV = 0	The investment would neither gain nor lose value from the firm	A deeper analysis should be undertaken using other different criteria or for any other reasons worth consideration

Example

VII. Cash flow

Cash flow - The balance of the amounts of cash received and paid by a business on a defined period of time of a specific project.

Uses of Cash Flow

1. To evaluate the state or performance of a business or project.

2. To determine problems with liquidity. Being profitable does not necessarily mean being liquid. A company can fail because of a shortage of cash, even while profitable.

3. To generate project rate of returns of cash-in and out flows.

4. To examine income or growth of a business.

Cash flows can be classified into:

1. **Operational cash flows:** Cash received or expended as a result of the company's core business activities.

2. **Investment cash flows**: Cash received or spent through capital expenditure, investments or acquisitions.

3. **Financing cash flows:** Cash received or spent as a result of financial activities.

All of the three together - the net cash flow - are necessary to reconcile the beginning cash balance to the ending cash balance. Loan draw downs or equity injections, that is just shifting of capital but no expenditure as such, are not considered in the net cash flow.

Operating Cash Flow – It is often referred to as working capital, is the cash flow generated from internal operations. It comes from sales of the product or service of your business, and because it is generated internally, it is under your control.

Investing Cash Flow - The internally generated cash flow from non-operating activities. This includes investments in plant and equipment or other fixed assets, nonrecurring gains or losses, or other sources and uses of cash outside of normal operations.

Financing Cash Flow - The externally generated financing cash flow such as: lenders, investors and shareholders. May be for the purpose: new loan, the repayment of a loan, the issuance of stock, and the payment of dividend are some of the activities included in the cash flow statement.

Common methods include:

a) Sales

b) Inventory

c) Sales Commissions

d) Wages

e) Maintenance

f) Equipment Leases or buy it

g) Rent, sale or lease back

h) Research & Development

i) Consulting Fees

j) Interest

k) Taxes

Benefits from using cash flow

The cash flow statement is one of the four main financial statements of a company. The cash flow statement can be examined to determine the short-term sustainability of a company. If cash is increasing (and operational cash flow is positive), then a company will often be deemed to be healthy in the short-term.

Increasing or stable cash balances suggest that a company is able to meet its cash needs, and remain solvent. This information cannot always be seen in the income statement or the balance sheet of a company. For instance, a company may be generating profit, but still have difficulty in remaining solvent.

Example of a positive P4,000 cash flow

Transaction	In (Debit)	Out (Credit)
Incoming Loan	+ P5,000	
Sales (Cash)	+ P3,000	
Materials		P1,000
Labor		P1,000
Purchased Capital		P1,000
Loan Repayment		P 500
Taxes		P 500
Total Cash Flow		+P4,000

In this example the following types of flows are included:

1. Incoming loan: financial flow

2. Sales: operational flow

3. Materials: operational flow

4. Labor: operational flow

5. Purchased Capital: Investment flow

6. Loan Repayment: financial flow

7. Taxes: financial flow

Example - Compare two firms using only total cash flow and then separate cash flow streams. The last three years show the following total cash flows:

Company A:

Year 1: cash flow of +10M

Year 2: cash flow of +11M

Year 3: cash flow of +12M

Company B:

Year 1: cash flow of +15M

Year 2: cash flow of +16M

Year 3: cash flow of +17M

Company B has a higher yearly cash flow and looks like a better one in which to invest.

Now let us see how their cash flows are made up:

Company A:

Year 1: OC: +20M FC: +5M IC: -15M, total = +10M

Year 2: OC: +21M FC: +5M IC: -15M, total = +11M

Year 3: OC: +22M FC: +5M IC: -15M, total = +12M

Company B:

Year 1: OC: +10M FC: +5M IC: 0, total = +15M

Year 2: OC: +11M FC: +5M IC: 0, total = +16M

Year 3: OC: +12M FC: +5M IC: 0, total = +17M

OC = Operational Cash,

FC = Financial Cash,

IC = Investment Cash

Now it shows that Company A is actually earning more cash by its core activities and has already spent 45M in long term investments, of which the revenues will only show up after three years. When comparing investments using cash flows always make sure to use the same cash flow layout.

VIII. Break-Even Point

The **break-even point (BEP)** represents the sales amount in either unit or revenue terms that is required to cover total costs (both fixed and variable). Total profit at the break-even point is zero.

The break-even point (BEP) in economics and business is the point at which total cost and total revenue are equal. In short, all costs that need to be paid are paid by the firm but the profit is equal to 0.

Any of these would reduce the break-even point. In other words, the business would not need to sell so many tables to make sure it could pay its fixed costs.

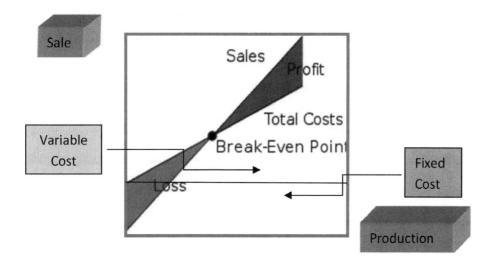

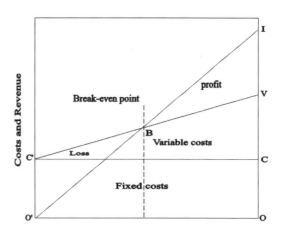

The Purpose:

The main purpose of **break-even analysis** is to determine the minimum output that must be exceeded in order to make profit. It also is a rough indicator of the earnings impact of a marketing activity.

Example:

The direct labor cost and material cost of a certain product are sold P P500 and P700 per unit, respectively. Fixed charges are P 100,000 per month and other variable costs are P 100 per unit. If the product is sold at P1,400 per unit, how many units must be produced and sold to break-even?

Solution:

X = number of units produced per month to break-even

Expenses:

Direct labor cost	= 500X
Direct material cost	= 700X
Variable cost	= 100X
Fixed charges	= 100,000

Solution

Total expenses	= 500X + 700X + 100X + 100,000
Total expenses	= 1,300X + 100,000
Total income	= 1,400X

1300X +100,000

To break even

Total income	= Total expenses
1,400X	= 1,300X + 100,000
X(1,400 – 1300)	= 100,000
100X	= 100,000

X = 1000 units to be sold as to break-even

IX. Cost of capital

The cost of capital is the cost of a company's funds from an investor's point of view. It is used to evaluate new projects of a company. It is the minimum return that investors expect for providing capital to the company, thus setting a benchmark that a new project has to meet.

Basic concept

For an investment to be worthwhile, the expected return on capital has to be higher than the cost of capital. Given a number of competing investment opportunities, investors are expected to put their capital to work in order to maximize the return.

In other words, the cost of capital is the rate of return that capital could be expected to earn in the best alternative investment of equivalent risk. If a project is of similar risk to a company's average business activities it is reasonable to use the company's average cost of capital as a basis for the evaluation. However, for projects outside the core business of the company, the current cost of capital may not be the appropriate yardstick to use, as the risks of the businesses are not the same.

A company's securities typically include both debt and equity, one must therefore calculate both the cost of debt and the cost of equity to determine a company's cost of capital. Importantly, both cost of debt and equity must be forward looking, and reflect the expectations of risk and return in the future.

This means, for instance, that the past cost of debt is not a good indicator of the actual forward looking cost of debt.

Once cost of debt and cost of equity have been determined the weighted average cost of capital (WACC), can be calculated. This WACC can then be used as a discount rate for a project's projected cash flows.

Cost of debt

When companies borrow funds from outside or take debt from financial institutions or other resources the interest paid on that amount is called cost of debt. The cost of debt is computed by taking the rate on a risk-free bond whose duration matches the term structure of the corporate debt, then adding a default premium. This default premium will rise as the amount of debt increases (since, all other things being equal, the risk rises as the cost of debt rises.

Cost of capital

It refers to the opportunity cost of making a specific investment. It is the rate of return that could have been earned by putting the same money into a different investment with equal risk. Thus, the cost of capital is the rate of return required to persuade the investor to make a given investment. This is determined by the market and represents the degree of perceived risk by investors. When given the choice between two investments of equal risk, investors will generally choose the one providing the higher return.

X. Margin Of Safety

Margin of safety-financial and Margin of safety-safety margin

It is the difference between the intrinsic value and its market price. It is how much output or sales level can fall before a business reaches its breakeven point.

What is Margin of Safety

This is the principle of investing in which an investor only purchases significantly below its intrinsic value. In other words, when market price is significantly below your estimation of the intrinsic value, the difference is the margin of safety. This difference allows an investment to be made with minimal downside risk.

Determining a company's "true" worth, its intrinsic value is highly subjective. Each investor has a different way of calculating intrinsic value, which may or may not be correct. In addition, it's notoriously difficult to predict a company's earnings. Margin of safety provides a cushion against errors in calculation.

Formula: Margin of Safety = Budgeted Sales - Breakeven Sales

Example Problem :Margin of Safety

Current sales are P100,000

Break-even point is P75,000.

Margin of Safety or Safety Buffer

P25,000 = P100,000 - P75,000

In percentage = 25,000 / 100,000 = 25%

To express it as a percentage, the Margin of Safety needs to be divided by Budgeted sales. The margin of safety is a financial ratio that measures the amount of sales that exceed the break-even point. In other words, this is the revenue earned after the company or department pays all of its fixed and variable costs associated with producing the goods or services. You can think of it like the amount of sales a company can afford to lose before it stops being profitable.

It is called the safety margin because it's kind of like a buffer. This is the amount of sales that the company or department can lose before it starts losing money. As long as there's a buffer, by definition the operations are profitable. If the safety margin falls to zero, the operations break even for the period and no profit is realized. If the margin becomes negative, the operations lose money.

Management uses this calculation to judge the risk of a department, operation, or product. The smaller the percentage or number of units, the riskier the operation is because there's less room between profitability and loss. Let's take a look at how to calculate the margin of safety.

Example:

$$\text{Margin of Safety} = \frac{\text{Actual Sales}}{\text{Break-even Point}}$$

This formula shows the total number of sales above the breakeven point. In other words, the total number of sales that can be lost before the company loses money. Sometimes it's also helpful to express this calculation in the form of a percentage. We can do this by subtracting the break-even point from the current sales and dividing by the current sales.

Example:

$$\text{Margin of Safety} = \frac{\text{Actual Sales} - \text{Break-even Point}}{\text{Actual Sales}}$$

This version of the margin of safety equation expresses the buffer zone in terms of a percentage of sales. Management typically uses this form to analyze sales forecasts and ensure sales will not fall below the safety percentage.

Managerial accountants also tend to calculate the margin of safety in units by subtracting the breakeven point from the current sales and dividing the difference by the selling price per unit.

Example:

$$\text{Margin of Safety} = \frac{\text{Actual Sales} - \text{Break-even Point}}{\text{Selling Price Per Unit}}$$

This equation measures the profitability buffer zone in units produced and allows management to evaluate the production levels needed to achieve a profit. Let's take a look at an example.

Example

The margin of safety is a particularly important measurement for management when they are contemplating an expansion or new product line because it shows how safe the company is and how much lost sales or increased costs the company can absorb.

XI. Weighted Average Cost Of Capital

The **weighted average cost of capital (WACC)**

This is the rate a company is expected to pay on **average** to all its security holders to finance its assets. The **WACC** is commonly referred to as the firm's **cost of capital**. Importantly, it is dictated by the external market and not by management.

The Weighted Average Cost of Capital (WACC) serves as the discount rate for calculating the Net Present Value (NPV) of a business. It is also used to evaluate investment opportunities, as it is considered to represent the firm's opportunity cost.

The **weighted average cost of capital (WACC)** is the rate that a company is expected to pay to finance its assets. WACC is the minimum return that a company must earn on existing asset base to satisfy its creditors, owners, and other providers of capital.

The capitalization formula is the foundation of the Income Approach to business valuation. The weighted average cost of capital (WACC) used in the formula is a measure of the combined cost of capital of all the investors. A fundamental assumption in this formula is that the cash flow will be distributed, in each period, to all the investors in proportion to their holdings. Proportional distribution of cash flow may occur in some situations, however, it generally does not happen in leveraged acquisitions. In leveraged acquisitions debt holders have priority. They get paid interest and principal before dividends are paid to the equity holder. As a result, the equity holder's cash flow is pushed back in the future. There appears to be no discussion in the valuation field on how equity holder's return is impacted due to preferential distribution to the debt holder.

Analysis here shows that the actual return to the equity holder is significantly lower than the one used in calculating WACC due to priority of payments to debt holder. In other words, capitalization formula with WACC overvalues a business from the equity holder's perspective.

The Formula

Capitalization formula with weighted average cost of capital (WACC) is universally used in business valuation. It is quick and convenient. It is used by itself to value 100% of the business, or as part of the excess earnings method, or to calculate the Terminal Value in a DCF (Discounted Cash Flow) analysis. In DCF approach a large portion of the total value is usually based on the Terminal Value, which is calculated using the capitalization formula. However, there are certain, and potentially serious, problems in using the capitalization formula. This article discusses one such problem in detail i.e. the use of WACC. Other problems with the capitalization formula are also briefly discussed.

The capitalization formula has an implicit assumption that only the interest cost of debt is relevant to valuation. It ignores the impact of debt repayments to equity holder's cash flow. Valuation textbooks and literature do not appear to have explicit discussion on this subject. Many in the industry believe that debt repayment impact can be ignored because a typical business has a perpetual ability to continuously refinance the debt at no transaction cost, and that a constant debt to equity ratio can be maintained through additional borrowing as the business grows. Even if one were to assume unconstrained and perpetual access to debt refinancing, capitalization formula implicitly assumes that such debt refinancing proceeds are distributable, and are distributed, to the equity holder as dividend, such that each period's cash flow is distributed to each investor in proportion to their investment. Such luxury of perpetual debt, perpetual debt/equity ratio, and the option to distribute the refinancing proceeds as dividend, is not realistic for most situations. Therefore, this article analyses the impact of the preferential distribution of the debt interest and the debt principal repayment on the results of the capitalization formula. The analysis quantifies impact on value and impact on equity return as-if debt has to be repaid without new borrowing.

XII. Benefit/Cost Ratio

The method of selecting alternatives that is most commonly used by government agencies for analyzing the desirability of public projects is the benefit/cost ratio B/C) method of analysis is based on the ratio of the benefits to costs associated with a particular project.

B/C = BENEFITS - DISBENEFITS OVER COSTS

Benefits are advantages, expressed in terms of pesos which happen to the owner. On the other hand, when the project under consideration involves disadvantages to the owner, these are known as disbenefit.

The costs are the anticipated expenditures for construction, operation, maintenance, etc. A B/C ratio greater than or equal to 1.0 indicates that the project under consideration is economically advantages.

Example 1 - An investment of P1,500,000 in grants to develop new product. The grants would extend over a ten-year period and would achieve an estimated savings of P600,000 per year in its upgrading cost and other expenses. The program would be an addition to ongoing and planned activities, thus an estimated P175,000 a year would have to be released from other program as a developmental support. With a rate of return of 10% is expected. Shall the program be accepted?

Benefit = P600,000 per year

Disbenefit = P175,000 per year

$$PMT = PV[i\,/1-(1+i)^{-n}]$$

Solution:

Cost = P1,500,000 (A/P, 10%, 10) = P298,950 per year

= 1,500,000 x 0.10/ [1-(1.1)^-10)]

= P298,950 per year

B/C = P600,000 - P175,000 / P298,950 = 1.42

The project is justified, since B/C greater than 1.00

XIII. Profitability Index

The **profit investment ratio** and **value investment ratio**, is the ratio of payoff to investment of a proposed project. It is a useful tool for ranking projects because it allows you to quantify the amount of value created per unit of investment.

The ratio is calculated as follows:

$$\text{Profitability Index} = \frac{\text{PV of future cash flows}}{\text{Initial Investment}}$$

Assuming that the cash flow calculated does not include the investment made in the project, a profitability index of 1 indicates breakeven. As the value of the profitability index increases, so does the financial attractiveness of the proposed project.

Rules for selection or rejection of a project:

If PI > 1 then accept the project

If PI < 1 then reject the project

Example:

Investment: = 40,000

Life of the Machine: = 5 Years

Calculate Net present value at 10% and PI:

Cash Flow After Taxes

This is a measure of a company's cash flow after all taxes are paid. It is calculated by taking the net income and adding back in the value of all non cash expenses, notably amortization and depreciation publicly traded companies with a high cash flow after taxes are in a better position to distribute cash dividends than those with a low cash after taxes. In addition to this, it is also used as a measure of general performance and financial health.

CFAT Year	CFAT
1	18,000

1	12,000
3	10,000
4	9,000
5	6,000

Year	CFAT	PV@10%	PV	
				$PV = FV (1 + i)^{-n}$
1	18,000	0.909	16,362	
2	12,000	0.827	9,924	
3	10,000	0.752	7,520	
4	9,000	0.683	6,147	
5	6,000	0.621	3,726	
	Total present value		43,679	
	(-) Investment		40,000	
	NPV		3,679	

$PI = 43,679/40,000 = 1.091 > 1 \Rightarrow$ Accept the project

Profitability Index

Profitability index is an investment appraisal technique calculated by dividing the present value of future cash flows of a project by the initial investment required for the project.

The Formula

Present Value of Future Cash Flows

$$\text{Profitability Index} = \frac{\text{Present Value of Future Cash Flows}}{\text{Initial Investment Required}}$$

$$\text{Profitability Index} = 1 + \frac{\text{Net Present Value}}{\text{Initial Investment Required}}$$

Explanation

Profitability index is actually a modification of the net present value method.

While present value is an absolute measure (i.e. it gives as the total money figure for a project), the profitability index is a relative measure (i.e. it gives as the figure as a ratio).

Example

Company C is undertaking a project at a cost of P50 million which is expected to generate future net cash flows with a present value of P65 million. Calculate the profitability index.

Solution

PI = PV of Future Net Cash Flows / Initial Investment Required

Profitability Index = $65M / $50M = 1.3

NPV = PV of Net Future Cash Flows − Initial Investment Required

Net Present Value = 65M-50M = 15M.

The information about NPV and initial investment can be used to calculate profitability index as follows:

Profitability Index = 1 + (Net Present Value / Initial Investment Required)

Profitability Index = 1 + 15M / 5

XIV. Payback Period

The Payback Period is perhaps the simplest method of looking at one or more investment projects or ideas. The Payback Period method focuses on recovering the cost of investments. The Payback Period represents the amount of time that it takes for a capital budgeting project to recover its initial cost.

Payback Period. Formula

Calculate the Payback Period.

The Costs of Project / Investment

$$PP = \frac{\text{The Costs of Project / Investment}}{\text{Annual Cash Inflows}}$$

The Payback Period concept holds that all other things being equal, the better investment is the one with the shorter payback period.

Payback Period calculation

Example 1 - A project costing a total of P2,000,000. The expected returns of the project amount to P 400,000 annually. The Payback Period would be P 2,000,000 divided by P400,000 = 5 years.

Benefits of Payback Period

The advantage use of Payback Period certainly is its virtue of being easy to compute and easy to understand. But that simplicity carries weaknesses with it.

Limitations of the Payback Period

There are at least two major problems associated with the Payback Period model:

1. PP ignores any benefits that occur after the Payback Period. It does not measure total incomes.

2. PP ignores the time value of money.

Because of these two reasons, other financial methods of Capital budgeting are advisable.

The basic premise of the payback method is that the more quickly the cost of an investment can be recovered, the more desirable is the investment.

Formula:

$$\text{Payback period} = \frac{\text{Investment required}}{\text{Net Annual Cash Inflow}}$$

To illustrate the payback method:

Example 2 – A company is considering buying two machines. Machine A costs P 25,000 and will reduce operating cost by P 5,000 per year. Machine B costs only P 20,000 but will also reduce operating costs by P 5,000 per year.

Required:

a). Calculate payback period.

b). Which machine should be purchased according to payback method?

The Computation:

Machine A payback period = P 25,000 / P 5,000 = 5.0 years

Machine B payback period = P 20,000 / P 5,000 = 4.0 years

As calculated, this company should purchase machine B, since it has a shorter payback period than machine A.

1. Clearly, a main defect of the straight payback period method is that it ignores the time value of money principle, which, in turn, can produce unrealistic expectations.

2. A second drawback is that it ignores any benefits generated after the payback period, and thus a project that would return $1 million after, say, six years might be ranked lower than a project with a three-year payback that returns only $100,000 thereafter.

3. Another alternative to calculating by payback period is to develop an internal rate of return.

4. Under most analyses, projects with shorter payback periods rank higher than those with longer paybacks, even if the latter promise higher returns. Longer paybacks can be affected by such factors as market changes, changes in interest rates, and economic shifts. Shorter cash paybacks also enable companies to recoup an investment sooner and put it to work elsewhere.

5. Generally, a payback period of three years or less is desirable; if a project's payback period is less than a year, some contend it should be judged essential.

XV. Inflation

Inflation - The percentage change in the value of the Wholesale Price Index (WPI) a yearly basis. It effectively measures the change in the prices of a basket of goods and services in a year.

The Central Bank of the Philippines is in-charge to stop any severe inflation, along with severe deflation, in an attempt to keep the excessive growth of prices to a level.

The measure of Inflation and Interest Rates - Whenever you hear the latest inflation update on the news, chances are that interest rates are mentioned in the same breath. Inflation is a sustained increase in the general level of prices for goods and services.

When inflation goes up, there is a decline in the purchasing power of money. Variations on inflation include deflation, hyperinflation and stagflation.

Two theories as to the cause of inflation are demand-pull inflation and cost-push inflation. Inflation is measured with a price index. The two main groups of price indexes that measure inflation are the **Consumer Price Index and the Producer Price Indexes.**

In the long term, stocks are good protection against inflation. Inflation is a serious problem for fixed income investors. It's important to understand the difference between nominal interest rates and real interest rates.

Inflation = percentage change in the value of the Consumers Price Index

The formula

$$\text{Inflation} = \frac{\text{CP2} - \text{CP1}}{\text{CP1}} \times 100$$

CP2 in a month of current year

CPI in a same month of previous year

Example: To illustrate the method of calculation: January 2017 CPI was 221.07 and in January 2016 was 211.39

$$\text{Inflation} = \frac{221.07 - 211.39}{211.39} \times 100$$

Inflation = 4.58%

Inflation occurs due to an imbalance between demand and supply of money, changes in production and distribution cost or increase in taxes on products. When economy experiences inflation, i.e. when the price level of goods and services rises, the value of currency reduces. This means now each unit of currency buys fewer goods and services.

It has its worst impact on consumers. High prices of day-to-day goods make it difficult for consumers to afford even the basic commodities in life. This leaves them with no choice but to ask for higher incomes. Hence the government tries to keep inflation under control.

Contrary to its negative effects, a moderate level of inflation characterizes a good economy. An inflation rate of 2 or 3% is beneficial for an economy as it encourages people to buy more and borrow more, because during times of lower inflation, the level of interest rate also remains low. Hence, the government, as well as the central bank always strives to achieve a limited level of inflation.

In layman's terms, inflation refers to the value of your dollar. In periods of rising inflation, the dollar is worth less; however, in periods of declining inflation, the dollar is worth more. When researching investments or buying a house, it is a good idea to factor in the inflation rate to make a better assessment of your return. For example, a certificate of deposit that pays 3 percent over three years, with inflation rates at 3 percent, has the equivalent return of 0 percent.

Hyperinflation

If inflation is in the upward direction and gets totally out of control, it can grossly interfere with the normal workings of the economy, hurting its ability to supply goods. Hyperinflation can lead to the abandonment of the use of the country's currency.

High inflation increases the opportunity cost of holding cash balances and can induce people to hold a greater portion of their assets in interest paying accounts. However, since cash is still needed in order to carry out transactions this means that more bank withdrawals are necessary in order to make withdrawals.

With high inflation, firms must change their prices often in order to keep up with economy-wide changes. But often changing prices is itself a costly activity whether explicitly, as with the need to print new menus, or implicitly, as with the extra time and effort needed to change prices constantly.

Some Theories of inflation

When inflation goes up, there is a decline in the purchasing power of money. Variations on inflation include deflation, hyperinflation and stagflation. Two theories as to the cause of inflation are demand-pull inflation and cost-push inflation. When there is unanticipated inflation, creditors lose, people on a fixed-income lose, as uncertainty reduces spending and exporters aren't as competitive. Lack of inflation (or deflation) is not necessarily a good thing. Inflation is measured with a price index. The two main groups of price indexes that measure inflation are the Consumer Price Index and the Producer Price Indexes.

XVI. Repayment Plan

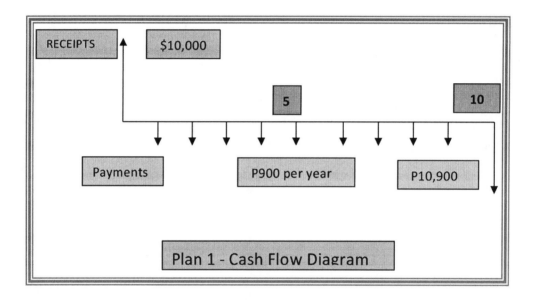

Plan 1 - Repayment of $10,000 in 10 years with interest at 9%

Plan 1 - This a series of equal payment only over time plus initial investment payment at the end of the term

END OF YEAR	INTEREST DUE (9% OF MONEY OWED AT START OF YEAR)	TOTAL MONEY OWED BEFORE YEAR-END PAYMENT	YEAR-END PAYMENT	MONEY OWED AFTER YEAR-END PAYMENT
0				10,000
1	900	10,000	900	10,000
2	900	10,000	900	10,000
3	900	10,000	900	10,000
4	900	10,000	900	10,000
5	900	10,000	900	10,000
6	900	10,000	900	10,000
7	900	10,000	900	10,000
8	900	10,000	900	10,000
9	900	10,000	900	10,000
10	900	10,000	10,900	0.000

TOTAL   **P19,000**

Advantages of this Plan1:

a). You need not worry of different releases of series of payments.

b). It's easy to make a payment trace back

c). There is no big chunk of payments made along the periods.

d). Residual revenues can be accessible for the period covered.

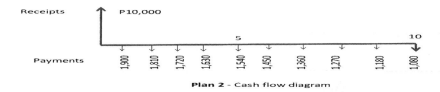

Plan 2 - Cash flow diagram

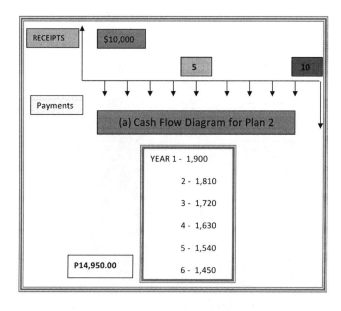

Plan 2 - Repayment of $10,000 in 10 years with interest at 9%

Plan 2 – A series of payment plus servicing of loan principal distributed throughout the term

END OF YEAR	INTEREST DUE (9% OF MONEY OWED AT START OF YEAR)	TOTAL MONEY OWED BEFORE YEAR-END PAYMENT	YEAR-END PAYMENT	MONEY OWED AFTER YEAR-END PAYMENT
0				10,000
1	900	10,900	1,900	9,000
2	810	9,810	1,810	8,000
3	720	8,720	1,720	7,000
4	630	7,630	1,630	6,000
5	540	6,540	1,540	5,000
6	450	5,450	1,450	4,000
7	360	4,360	1,360	3,000
8	270	3,270	1,270	2,000
9	180	2,180	1,180	1,000
10	90	1,090	1,090	0.000

TOTAL   **P14,950**

Advantages:

a). Fast diminishing of loan amount

b). Low overall amount servicing

c). Easy to calculate and monitor

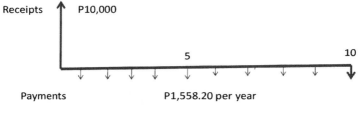

Plan 3 - Cash flow diagram

Plan 3 – Interest plus the equal servicing of the principal amount per period. This could come out as amortization or sinking fund method of loan servicing

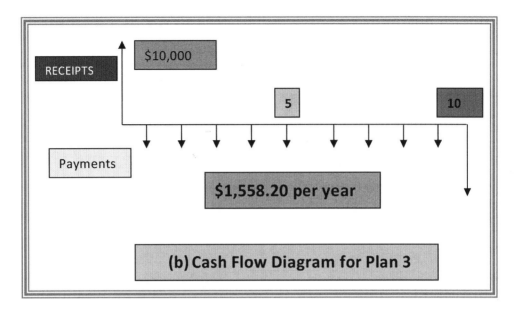

(b) Cash Flow Diagram for Plan 3

Plan 3 - Repayment of P10,000 in 10 years with interest at 9%

END OF YEAR	INTEREST DUE (9% OF MONEY OWED AT START OF YEAR	TOTAL MONEY OWED BEFORE YEAR-END PAYMENT	YEAR-END PAYMENT	MONEY OWED AFTER YEAR-END PAYMENT
0				10,000.00
1	900.00	10,900	1,558.20	9,341.80
2	840.76	10,182.56	1,558.20	8,624.36

3	776.19	9,400.55	1,558.20	7,842.35
4	705.81	8,548.16	1,558.20	6,989.96
5	629.10	7,619.06	1,558.20	6,060.86
6	545.46	6,606.32	1,558.20	5,048.12
7	454.33	5,502.45	1,558.20	3,944.25
8	354.98	4,299.23	1,558.20	2,741.03
9	246.69	2,987.72	1,558.20	1,429.52
10	128.66	1,558.18	1,558.18	0.00

TOTAL   P15,582.00

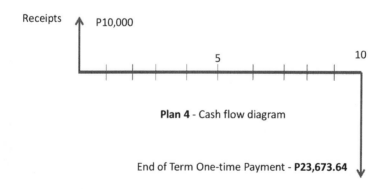

Plan 4 - Cash flow diagram

End of Term One-time Payment - **P23,673.64**

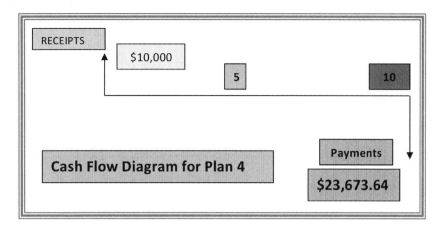

Plan 4 – A lump sum at the end of the term of Future versus the present value.

Plan 4 - Repayment of P10,000 in 10 years with interest at 9%

END OF YEAR	INTEREST DUE (9% OF MONEY OWED AT START OF YEAR)	TOTAL MONEY OWED BEFORE YEAR-END PAYMENT	YEAR-END PAYMENT	MONEY OWED AFTER YEAR-END PAYMENT
0			0.00	10,000.00
1	900.00	10,900.00	0.00	10,900.00

2	981.00	11,881.00	0.00	11,881.00
3	1,069.29	12,950.29	0.00	12,950.29
4	1,165.53	14,115.82	0.00	14,115.82
5	1,270.42	15,386.24	0.00	15,386.24
6	1,384.76	16,771.00	0.00	16,771.00
7	1,509.39	18,280.39	0.00	18,280.39
8	1,645.24	19,925.63	0.00	19,925.63
9	1,793.31	21,718.94	0.00	21,718.94
10	1,954.70	23,673.64	P23,673.64	0.00

XVII. Lease or buy decision

What is a Lease?

Lease vs Buy - A lease is a long term agreement to rent equipment, land, buildings, or any other asset. The user (lessee) makes periodic payments to the owner of the asset (lessor). The lease payment covers the original cost of the equipment or other asset and provides the lessor a profit.

Types of Leases

There are three major kinds of leases:

1. **Financial leases** are most common by far. A financial lease is usually written for a term not to exceed the economic life of the equipment. You will find that a financial lease usually provides that:

a). Periodic payments be made,

b). Ownership of the equipment reverts to the lessor at the end of the lease term,

c). The lease is non cancellable and the lessee has a legal obligation to continue payments to the end of the term, and

d). The lessee agrees to maintain the equipment.

2. **The operating lease,** or "maintenance lease," can usually be canceled under conditions spelled out in the lease agreement. Maintenance of the asset is usually the responsibility of the owner (lessor). Computer equipment is often leased under this kind of lease.

3. **The sale and leaseback** is similar to the financial lease. The owner of an asset sells it to another party and simultaneously leases it back to use it for a specified term. This arrangement lets you free the money tied up in an asset for use elsewhere. You'll find that buildings are often leased this way.

You may also hear leases described as net leases. Under a net lease the lessee is responsible for expenses such as those for maintenance, taxes, and insurance. The lessor pays these expenses under a gross lease. Financial leases are usually net leases.

The lease versus buy decision is based on a comparison between the net present value of the buy alternative with the net present value of the cash flows associated with leasing.

Leasing finances the *use* of a vehicle; buying with a loan finances the *purchase* of a vehicle. Each has its own benefits and drawbacks. When making a 'lease or buy' decision you must look not only at financial comparisons but also at your own personal priorities - what's important to you.

Is having a new vehicle every two or three years with no major repair risks more important than long-term cost? Or are long term cost savings more important than lower monthly payments? Is having some ownership in your vehicle more important than low up-front costs and no down payment? Is it important to you to pay off your vehicle and be debt-free for a while, even if it means higher monthly payments for the first few years?

So we find out that making a lease-or-buy decision is not quite cut and dry. There are trade-offs, pluses and minuses, pros and cons to consider.

When you buy, you pay for the *entire cost* of the vehicle, regardless of how many miles you drive it or how long you keep it. Monthly payments are higher than for leasing. You typically make a down payment, pay sales taxes in cash or roll them into your loan, and pay an interest rate determined by your loan company based on your credit score. You make your first payment a month after you sign your contract. Later, you may decide to sell or trade the vehicle for its depreciated resale or trade value.

When you lease, you pay only a *portion of a vehicle's cost*, which is the part that you "use up" during the time you're driving it. Leasing is a form of financing and is not the same as renting. You have the option of not making a down payment, you pay sales tax only on your monthly payments (in most states), and you pay a financial rate, called *money factor*, that is similar to the interest on a loan. You may also be required to pay fees and possibly a *security deposit* that you don't pay when you buy. You make your first payment at the time you sign your contract — for the month ahead. At lease-end, you may either return the vehicle, or purchase it for its *depreciated* resale value. You may be charged a lease-end *disposition* fee.

Example:

if you **LEASE** a P1,500,000 car that will have, say, an estimated resale value of P900,000 after 24 months, you only pay for the P600,000 difference (this is called *depreciation*), plus finance charges, plus possible fees. You return the car at lease-end, or buy it to own it.

When you **BUY**, you pay the entire P1,500,000, plus finance charges, plus possible fees. You own the car at the end of your loan, although its value is less than the P1,500,000 you initially paid.

This difference is fundamentally why leasing offers significantly lower monthly payments than buying.

Kinds of Lessors

Commercial banks, insurance companies, and finance companies do most of the leasing. Many of these organizations have formed subsidiaries primarily concerned with equipment leasing. These subsidiaries are usually capable of making lease arrangements for almost anything.

In addition to financial organizations, there are companies which specialize in leasing. Some are engaged in general leasing, dealing with just about any kind of equipment. Others specialize in particular equipment, such as trucks or computers.

Advantages of Leasing Equipment

The obvious advantage to leasing is acquiring the use of an asset without making a large initial cash outlay. Compared to a loan arrangement to purchase the same equipment, a lease usually

1. requires no down payment, while a loan often requires 25 percent down;

2. Requires no restriction on a company's financial operations, while loans often do;

3. Spreads payments over a longer period (which means they'll be lower) than loans permit; and

4. Provides protections against the risk of equipment obsolescence, since the lessee can get rid of the equipment at the end of the lease.

There may also tax benefits in leasing. Lease payments are deductible as operating expenses if the arrangement is a true lease. Ownership, however, usually has greater tax advantages through depreciation. Naturally, you need to have enough income and resulting tax liability to take advantage of those two benefits.

Leasing has the further advantage that the leasing firm has acquired considerable knowledge about the kinds of equipment it leases. Thus, it can provide expert technical advice based on experience with the leased equipment.

Disadvantages of Leasing

In the first place, leasing usually costs more because you lose certain tax advantages that go with ownership of an asset. Leasing may not, however, cost more if you couldn't take advantage of those benefits because you don't have enough tax liability for them to come into play.

Obviously, you also lose the economic value of the asset at the end of the lease term, since you don't own the asset. Lessees have been known to grossly underestimate the salvage value of an asset. If they had known this value from the outset, they might have decided to buy instead of lease.

Further, you must never forget that a lease is a long-term legal obligation. Usually you can't cancel a lease agreement. So, it you were to end an operation that used leased equipment, you might find you'd still have to pay as much as if you had used the equipment for the full term of the lease.

Cost Analysis of Lease v. Loan/Purchase

You can analyze the costs of the lease versus purchase problem through discounted cash flow analysis. This analysis compares the cost of each alternative by considering: the timing of payments, tax benefits, interest rate on a loan, lease rate, and other financial arrangements.

To make the analysis you must first make certain assumptions about the economic life of the equipment, salvage value, and depreciation.

A straight cash purchase using a firm's existing funds will almost always be more expensive than the lease or loan/buy options because of the loss of use of the funds. Besides, most small firms don't have the large amounts of cash needed for major capital asset acquisitions in the first place.

To evaluate a lease you must first find the net cash outlay (not cash flow) in each year of the lease term. You find these amounts by subtracting the tax savings from the lease payment. This calculation gives you the net cash outlay for each year of the leases.

Each year's net cash outlay must next be discounted to take into account the time value of money. This discounting gives you the present value of each of the amounts.

The present value of an amount of money is the sum you would have to invest today at a stated rate of interest to have that amount of money at a specified future date. Say someone offered to give you $100 five years from now. How much could you take today and be as well off?

Common sense tells you could take less than $100, because you'd have the use of the money for the five year period. Naturally, how much less you could take depends on the interest rate you thought you could get if you invested the lesser amount.

Example: to have $1,000 five years from now at six percent compounded annually, you'd have to invest $747.260 today.

At 10 percent, you could take $620.92 now and have the $1000 at the end of five years.

$$\text{Present Value} = \frac{\text{Future Value}}{(1+i)^n} = \frac{P1000}{(1.06)^5} = P747.26$$

Look Before You Lease

A lease agreement is a legal document. It carries a long term obligation. You must be thoroughly informed of just what you're committing yourself to. Find out the lessor's financial condition and reputation. Be reasonably sure that the lease arrangements are the best you can get, that the equipment is what you need, and that the term is what you want. Remember, once the agreement is struck, it's just about impossible to change it.

The lease document will spell out the precise provisions of the agreement. Agreements may differ, but the major items will include:

- The specific nature of the financing agreement,

- Payment amount,

- Term of agreement,

- Disposition of the asset at the end of the term,

- Schedule of the value of the equipment for insurance and settlement purposes in case of damage or destruction,

- Who is responsible for maintenance and taxes,

- Renewal options,

- Cancellation penalties

XVIII. Gross Income Multiplier

The Gross Income Multiplier (GIM) or Gross Rent Multiplier indicates how many times the price/value of the property is greater than the gross income as computed for the owner.

The two concepts of gross income in the real estate industry:

1. Potential Gross Income (PGI)

2. Effective Gross Income (EGI

Within this context, there are also two respective multipliers that involve a property's gross income:

1. The Potential Gross Income Multiplier (PGIM)

2. The Effective Gross Income Multiplier (EGIM).

The formula:

$$EGIM = \frac{Market\ Price}{Effective\ Gross\ Income\ (EGI)}$$

Effective Gross Income (EGI):

EGI = Potential Gross Rental Income + Other Income

– Vacancy & Bad Debt Allowance

Calculate the EGIM on an annual basis. Thus, the annual Effective Gross Income is typically used in this formula. If a monthly EGIM is desired then the monthly EGI should be used.

The Potential Gross Income in the EGI formula includes primarily rental income and accounts also for any other income that may be produced by the property, such as income from vending machines, laundry room, parking, etc.

The vacancy accounts for space/units that remain vacant during the year and, as such do not actually provide any rental income to the landlord, while bad debt allowances cover any rent that is owed during the year but is not paid by the tenants with standing contracts.

Example

Calculate: Effective Gross Income and the respective annual EGIM.

Given:

Potential Gross Rental Income	= P500,000
Vacancy and Bad Debt Allowance (8%)	= P45,000
Other Income	= P35,000
Market Price	= P5,500,000

Solution:

Effective Gross Income = 500,000 + 35,000 – 45,000 = 490,000

EGIM = 5,500,000/490,000,000 =11.22

In this example, the asking price is 11.22 times greater than the effective gross income produced by the property. This indicates and goes to show that it is of too much an asking price.

Do some market value analysis for each property purchased. The Gross Rental Multiplier (GRM) is easy to calculate, but isn't a very precise tool for ascertaining value. However, it is an excellent first quick value assessment tool to see if further more detailed analysis is warranted. If the GRM is way out high or low compared to recent comparable sold properties, it probably indicates a problem with the property or gross over-pricing.

Research: GRM for recent sold properties:

Example:

Market Value/Annual Gross Income

= Gross Rent Multiplier (GRM)

Property sold for P800,000 / P120,000 Annual Income

= GRM of 6.67

Estimate value of property based on GRM:

Let's say that you did an analysis of recent comparable sold properties and found that, like the one above, their GRM's averaged around 6.80. Now you want to approximate the value of the property being considered for purchase. You know that its gross rental income is P70,000 annually.

GRM x Annual Income = Market Value

6.80 x P70,000 = P476,000

If it's listed for sale at P725,000 you might not want to waste more time in looking at it for purchase.

Don't get too reliant on this calculation, but it can be used to narrow down a crowded field of possible properties. This approach of calculation of GIM or the formula that determines the value of rental real estate and in used for a long, long time. Always use this only as a rule of thumb. Industry tells us not to invest in a property with a GIM of more than 8.

This helps the buyer open their eyes to mow much of a rental property they can afford to buy. It makes plenty of sense really. It seems that if a property was selling for 6 times the rental income, then that was a really good deal, anything higher than 8 times the rental income is something to think about again by use of other added analytical tools.

The GIM will constantly be in flux due to market changes and in other words, you must also consider interest rates and how that will influence the value. Also, every property is different and has different needs to be a viable rental. This means just plain different expenses for different properties, whether higher maintenance costs, insurance premiums, or whatever. The gross rent doesn't say much about the factor that really makes a rental property valuable: the net income.

This is what the valuation should be based upon, not other factors. This is one reason why a capitalization rate, or "cap rate" to determine value should be used. Simply explained the cap rate is the rate of return expected, or the rate of return on a property at a given price.

For instance, let's begin with the gross income of a property and subtract all expenses, but not loan payments. For this property, let's say the gross income is P90,000 per year, and the expenses are P38,000 you have net income before debt-service of P52,000 It will be important to apply the capitalization rate to this figure because the debt to income ratio will impede upon the value.

Let's say that for your area of the country, the normal capitalization rate is .10 or a 10% return on the value of the investment. It may be possible that the rate is higher making it more difficult for you to buy anything but let's see. Now divide the net income of P52,000 by .10, and you get P520,000 - the estimated value of the building. With a cap rate of .08, meaning an 8% return, the value would be P650,000

You could also consider that the cap rate is supported by the fair market asking price of the property based on comparables of the area. For this, just divide the net income by the asking price.

For example: A seller wants P2,500,000 for a property, and the net income is P225,000 you would divide P125,000 by P2,500,000 This gives you a cap rate of 0.09

A rule of thumb for evaluating the reasonableness of an asking price. One compares the monthly or annual gross income to the asking price and evaluates how that compares to typical ratios for similar properties.

Example: An investor will not pay more than 100 times the monthly gross income for a property. If a house rents for P120,000 per month, the investor will pay P1,200,000 but no more. The method is not a good indication of value and would never be employed by an appraiser, but it has its uses as a preliminary qualifier.

XIX. Modified Internal Rate Of Return (MIRR)

What is 'Modified Internal Rate Of Return - MIRR'

Modified internal rate of return (MIRR) assumes that positive cash flows are reinvested at the firm's cost of capital, and the initial outlays are financed at the firm's financing cost. By contrast, the traditional internal rate of return (IRR) assumes the cash flows from a project are reinvested at the IRR.

The MIRR more accurately reflects the cost and profitability of a project.

Example:

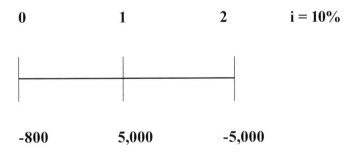

0	1	2	i = 10%
-800	5,000	-5,000	

This is a non-even cash flow stream

Therefore, let us solve for the MIRR

Steps to take:

1). Calculate the PV of outflows at 10%

$= (-800 \times 1) -5000/1 + 0.10)^2$

$= 4,932.23$

2). Calculate the FV of inflows at 10%

$= 5000 (1.10)$

$= 5,500$

3). Solve the PV outflows with the PV of FV of inflows

And solve for **k**

Solution:

$4932.23 = 5500 / (1 + k)^2$

$(1 + k)^2 = 5500 / 4932.23$

$1 + k = [5500 / 4932.23]^{\wedge} \frac{1}{2}$

$k = [5500 / 4932.23]^{\wedge} \frac{1}{2} - 1$

$= 0.0559$

$= 5.59\%$ as modified internal rate of return (MIRR)

XX. Supply And Demand

Demand

Demand is a need, want or desire for services or products by an accepted means to purchase it either by barter, trade-off or money. In economic analysis, demand is always based on the ability where it is ready, willing and able to make a purchase. Demand is inversely proportional to the selling price. Increase the price makes the demand lesser; Decrease the price makes the demand higher, as shown on the above graph.

The price P of a product is determined by a balance between production at each price (supply S) and the desires of those with purchasing power at each price (demand D).

The diagram shows a positive shift in demand from D_1 to D_2, resulting in an increase in price (P) and quantity sold (Q) of the product.

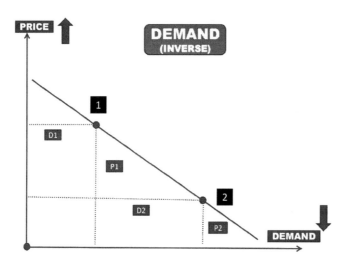

Make an assumption that it is on a linear function between the relationship of price and demand. At point 1, selling price of P_1 is high as demand D_1 is low. Nonetheless, at point 2, where P_2 Price is low but demand D_2 is high.

Therefore, demand is inversely proportional to the selling

Supply

Supply - is the amount of product or services made available for transaction.

When the selling price is high, more producers focus on higher production to achieve a better benefit for higher profit. However, if the selling price for a product declines, Developer-investors will not produced as much because of a meager profit

Therefore, the relationship between price and supply is that they are directly proportional: the higher the selling price, the more the supply; and the lesser the selling price, the lesser price is the supply.

Graph 2 below illustrates the price-supply

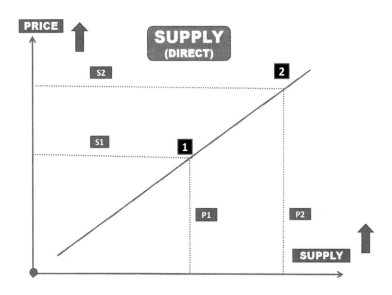

Demand and Supply

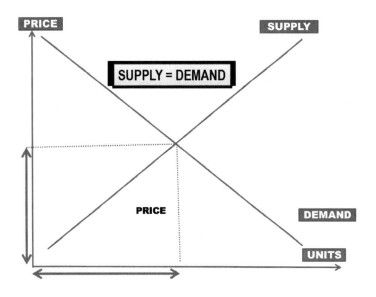

As shown on the graph below supply is equivalent to the demand

Supply is equal to demand thereby creating a perfect competition

Perfect competition – a type of market situation characterized by the following:

1. Many sellers and many buyers

2. Homogeneous products

3. Free market-entry and exit

4. Perfect information

5. Absence of all economic friction

As shown on the graph below: When there is additional supply without an additional demand, a new and lower price is established

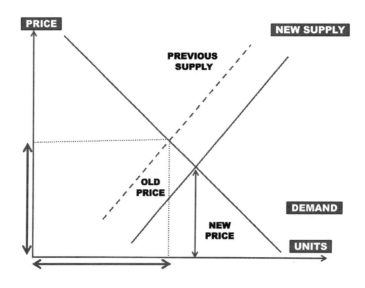

As shown on the graph below: There is additional demand without an additional supply, a new and higher price is established.

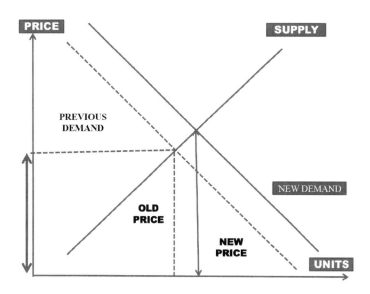

It concludes that in a competitive market, the unit price for a particular good, or other traded item such as land, labor or building, will vary until it settles at a point where the quantity demanded (at the current price) will equal the quantity supplied (at the current price), resulting in an **economic equilibrium** for price and quantity transacted.

Since determinants of supply and demand other than the price of the goods in question are not explicitly represented in the supply-demand diagram, changes in the values of these variables are represented by moving the supply and demand curves (often described as "shifts" in the curves).

Table 4-1 of Real Estate Business Supply and Demand

MARKET	SELLER	BUYER
Perfect Competition	Many	Many
Monopoly	One	Many
Monopsony	Many	One
Bilateral Monopoly	One	One
Duopoly	Two	Two
Duopoly	Two	Many
Duopsony	Many	Two
Oligopoly	Few	Many
Oligopsony	Many	Few
Bilateral Oligopoly	Few	Few

Under the assumption of **perfect competition,** supply is determined by marginal cost. That is, firms will produce additional output while the cost of producing an extra unit of output is less than the price they would receive.

The determinants of demand are:

1. Income.

2. Tastes and preferences.

3. Prices of related goods and services.

4. Consumers' expectations about future prices and incomes that can be checked.

5. Number of potential consumers.

Equilibrium

Generally speaking, an equilibrium is defined to be the price-quantity pair where the quantity demanded is equal to the quantity supplied. It is represented by the intersection of the demand and supply curves.

Market Equilibrium - A situation in a market when the price is such that the quantity demanded by consumers is correctly balanced by the quantity that firms wish to supply. In this situation, clearly, the market is in perfect competition.

hapter Six

XXI. Assessment

The Real Estate Appraisal and business valuation Investment Tools chapter is with arrays of chapter summary templates. To the students, professionals, bankers, lenders and investors: Should something hampers our decision on basic of real estate appraisal investment tools. Let us just visit our undertakings in this chapter:

Again, mathematics as well as appraisal always comes an easy connectivity to other economics and finance sciences. In business formulation and decision makings, appraisal is the main thing so powerful process for personal and business plan. The process of setting goals helps you choose where you want to go in life and in your new business venture. By knowing precisely what you want to achieve, you know where you will have to concentrate your efforts. You'll also quickly spot the distractions that would otherwise lure you from your course.

The sequence of getting into the core of real estate appraisal through the use of different investment tools:

INVESTMENT TOOLS

Financial Ratios	Statistics	Internal Rate of Return	Net Present Value	Cash Flow
Break-even Point	Cost of Capital	Margin of Safety	WACC	Benefit-Cost Ratio
Profitability Index	Payback Period	Inflation	Repayment Plan	Lease-Buy Decision
Income Multiplier	Supply - demand	Depreciation	Consultant Negotiation	Terms of Reference

NET PRESENT VALUE ELABORATION:

A capital expenditure project that is calculated to give positive NPV return is an attractive project. Money has a time value because of its investment opportunities.

Capital expenditure - funds used by a company to acquire, upgrade, and maintain physical assets such as property, industrial buildings, or equipment, often used to undertake new projects or investments by the firm.

A *capital budget* is used to evaluate potential investments or *expenditures* for specific projects or purposes.

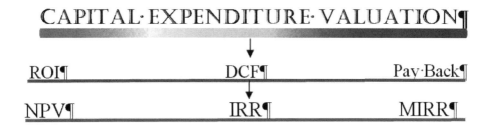

**HAPTER SEVEN**

BUSINESS VALUATION

*I think it will be found that experience, the true source and foundation of all knowledge, invariably confirms its truth.- **Thomas Malthus***

I. OBJECTIVE, PURPOSE AND APPROACH

➤ To know the fundamental differences between real estate appraisal and business valuation

➤ To develop a knack for business intricacies and develop it to a positive direction

➤ To correlate the advantages and disadvantages of valuation and appraisal methods

➤ To establish an environment conducive towards an in-depth investor's analysis.

➤ To allow the opportunity to identify on time and effort spent

➤ To introduce the life skills necessary to be successful in quality services

After this chapter, you will have learned:

❖ You will know the basic concept of real estate math for an interesting and understanding problems solving as an critical tools thorough analysis,

❖ How to present to business clients different financial comparative approaches to make

❖ How to knowledgeably sell, persuade and convince your clients on the service or product you present.

II. Business Valuation Organizations

Business Valuation Standards (BVS) – Sets of practices that are used in engineering, finance, real estate and economics industries.

The three major United States valuation societies:

- American Society of Appraisers (ASA),

- Institute of Business Appraisers (IBA), and

- National Association of Certified Valuation Analysts (NACVA)

Business Value Standard defines the measure of value used in business valuation. A number of business value standards are commonly used in appraising the value of businesses and professional practices, with fair market value, similar in real estate could perhaps the best known approach.

Philippine Valuation Standard (PVS) – This is the guidelines use in the practice of real estate appraisal and business valuation in the Philippines. The concept principles and guidelines:

- To promote and maintain a high level of public trust in appraisal practice.

- To help improve and standardize operation of assessment offices.

- To improve the productivity and equity of the tax base for property taxation purposes.

- To help contribute to the viability of the land/property market.

Subsequently, related to different pattern of standards from the following:

❖ Asean Valuation Standards (AVS)

❖ Uniform Standards of Professional Appraisal Practice (USPAP)

❖ International Association of Appraising Officers (IAAO) Standards

❖ International Valuation Standards (IVS)

❖ API and NZPI Standards

III. Business Valuation Definition

Business valuation – It is a process and a set of procedures used to estimate the economic value of an owner's interest in a business. Valuation is used for value formation to determine and estimate for a buyer and a particular seller that both are willing to pay or receive to consummate a sale of a business.

Fair market value - (FMV) is the foremost standard of measuring business value. It is defined differently by number of sources. Price is what you pay, value is what you get.

The State or government defines FMV as the price at which property would change hands between a willing buyer and a willing seller when the former is not under any compulsion to buy and the latter is not under any compulsion to sell. And both parties must have reasonable knowledge of relevant facts. This continues to be the prevailing definition of the fair market value.

There are three (3) generally accepted approaches to estimating value in a business enterprise and appraisal engagement. These are briefly described as follows.

Asset Approach - A generally accepted approach of a value formation indication of a business by using one or more methods based on the value of the subject business's assets net of all liabilities.

A going concern asset-based approach lists the business net balance sheet value of its assets and subtracts the value of its liabilities.

A **liquidation asset-based approach** determines the net cash that would be received if all assets were sold and liabilities paid off.

Market Approach – It is a generally accepted approach of value formation indication of a business. This is by using one or more methods that compare the subject business to similar businesses that have been sold in an open market.

Income Approach – This is the generally accepted approach of a value formation indication of a business using one or more methods that convert the anticipated economic benefits into a present value amount.

Conditions and Assumptions – assumptions and limiting conditions is a narration of the methods and what the valuer is not within the scope of his or her expertise on which the valuation is based. These typically include matters such as: accuracy of the value of the business based on the going concerns and iterations data as reflected on the financial statements. Factual information gathered must be accurate, and other such matters.

IV. Ethics Feature

All of the standards have a requirement of independence:

➢ The appraiser must not act in favor of the client or any other party.

➢ The valuation fees be not contingent on appraised value

➢ Fees based upon a percentage of the valuation are unethical and are not allowed and must be explicitly stated in the limiting conditions.

➢ The client must be informed of all assumptions made as part of the valuation.

➢ All liens, encumbrances and annotations must be a part of the valuation, unless otherwise explicitly stated in the limiting conditions.

➢ All professionals participating in a valuation report must sign it, and must have certification of their independence, fee arrangements, and other factors.

➢ Adhere to strict confidentiality of disclosure

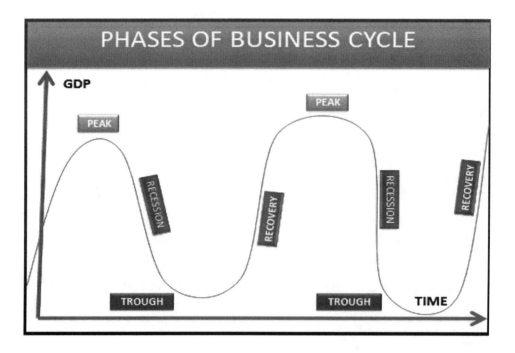

V. Business Life-Cycle - as an indicative measure of the business for sale

1. **Start up -** This is when a business first comes into the market. The market if fairly new and is not fully developed or serviced.

2. **Growth** – Time when a business begins experiencing positive fast growth. The business will expand its operations, hire new people, and possibly move into new markets and territories.

3. **Peak** – Time when a business begins to level up. Competitors are entering the market to challenge the leader. To remain competitive, the business must tighten its operations, increase productivity, and shed unprofitable operations.

4. **Decline -** This is when the business begins to decline due to competitive pressures from more capital-intensive competitors or when markets change.

The best of time to sell is right at the end of a business **growth**, just before entering into **peak**. You will be in a position of strength to command the best price for your business.

The better of time to sell is when you are at the front-half of number 3. The maturity stage for a business can operate for many years and you can command a good selling price if you hold a dominant position in the market.

The bad of time to sell is when the business is in a **decline**. Under these circumstances, the business owner generally sells the assets of the company and exits the business.

Strategize your plan to sell when you plan retirement from business or for any other reasons. Just do not leave your business too late. Simply put, watch your markets.

VI. Business Valuation Uses

Reasons why business valuation are required:

- ❖ Accounting & Financial

- ❖ Mergers & Acquisitions

- ❖ Allocation of Purchase Price

- ❖ Buy/Sell Agreements

- ❖ Corporate Planning

- ❖ Divestitures

- ❖ Estate Planning

- ❖ Estate Tax

- ❖ Financing

- ❖ Gift Tax

VII. Reasons for Selling

The most common reasons for selling

- ➢ Age/Retirement

- ➢ Burnout

- ➢ Boredom

- ➢ Financial and short of operating capital

- ➢ Technology inadequacy

- ➢ Diversification

- ➢ Family circumstances

- ➢ Market competition

- ➢ Health reasons

- ➢ Time for a change

A business for sale in a growing economy brings a higher price than selling in a recession. The best thing to do during a business decline or economic melt- down is preparing your company to achieve maximum value when the economy turns around.

VIII. Potential Clients

Who is your potential buyer?

- ➢ A corporate manager who knows the business and are ready to leave his job. These buyers often request a transition period where the seller will be engaged for up to a year helping the buyer assume the full transfer of the business. The seller is usually paid a fee for these services.

➢ Competitors may buy your business especially if you have a market niche or product-line that they want.

➢ Sometimes it is financially feasible to buy an existing operation than to take the time and expense to build one up. This is the job of business valuers as prudence and experience indicate so.

➢ Buying you out will depend on the strength of your market position. The stronger the market position, the more likely the buyout.

➢ The competition can secure the financing to buy you out. They may engage your services for a period to ensure your customers remain loyal to them.

IX. Buyers Motivation

Different motivations of a buyer

A valuable business is one that delivers both quality and quantity of its operational gains:

➢ 1. Business opportunity in a defined markets

➢ 2. Business with a strong marketing location

➢ 3. Business operating in a good economic growth trend market

➢ 4. Business with upward sales trends

➢ 5. business with strong financial profitability

➢ 6. Business with solid cash flows

Some indicators that proves a business is attractive:

➢ Situated in an densely populated prime location

➢ Solid supply of raw materials

➢ Less operation employees

➢ Better business environment

➢ Enhanced government support

➢ Attractive Livability indicators in the area of neighborhood

Confidentiality structure

The decision to sell your business should be kept among yourselves and other select individuals for the obvious reasons not to disrupt their working environment. Employees need not know the going concern negotiations. Any rumors of a sale can be unsettling for any staff. They may be feeling insecure with their jobs. Their efficiency and job effectiveness may get hampered.

X. Book Value

BOOK VALUE - The small business valuation based upon the accounting books of the business. Assets less liabilities equal the owner's equity, which is the "Book Value" of the business. The problem with book value small business valuation methods is that the accounting records may not accurately reflect the true value of the assets in the small business valuation.

Tangible Book Value - Business valuation is different than book value in that it deducts from asset value intangible assets, which are assets that are not hard (e.g., goodwill, patents, capitalized start-up expenses and deferred financing costs).

XI. The Formula

OWNER'S EQUITY = ASSETS - LIABILITIES

OWNER'S EQUITY = ASSETS – (goodwill, patents, capitalized start-up expenses and deferred financing costs) **- LIABILITIES**

Economic Book Value small business valuation allows for a value analysis that may adjust the assets to their market value. This small business valuation allows valuation of goodwill, real estate, inventories and other assets at their market value. This is where physical depreciation comes into the analysis.

XII. Income Capitalization Valuation Methods

First you must determine the capitalization rate - a rate of return required to take on the risk of operating the business (the riskier the business, the higher the required return). Earnings are then divided by that capitalization rate. The earnings figure to be capitalized should be one that reflects the true nature of the business, such as the last three years average, current year or projected year. When determining a capitalization rate you should compare with rates available to similarly risky investments.

$$\text{Business Value} = \frac{\text{Net Operating Income (NOI)}}{\text{Capitalization Rate}}$$

XIII. Problems Solving

Example 1 Find the business value of Firm A: Net Operating Income is P150,000 and capitalization rate is 15%, while Firm B with same NOI but with a Capitalization rate of 10%. Which firm has a higher business value?

Firm A @ 15%

$$\text{Business Value} = \frac{\text{Net Operating Income (NOI)}}{\text{Capitalization Rate}} = \frac{\text{P150,000}}{15\%}$$

Business Value = P10,000,000

Firm B @ 10%

$$\text{Business Value} = \frac{\text{Net Operating Income (NOI)}}{\text{Capitalization Rate}} = \frac{\text{P150,000}}{15\%}$$

Business Value = P15,000,000

Therefore: The higher the capitalization rate, the lower is the business value

Example 2 - A real estate developer made a capital investment of P15,000,000 for a mini mall and an estimated working capital of P2,000,000 is needed. It has an Annual depreciation estimated to be 10% of the fixed capital investment. Determine the rate of return on the total investment if the annual profit is P2,500,000

$$\text{Business Value} = \frac{\text{Net Operating Income (NOI)}}{\text{Capitalization Rate}}$$

or

$$\text{Capitalization Rate} = \frac{\text{Profit}}{\text{Total Capital Invested}}$$

$$\text{Capitalization Rate} = \frac{2,500,000}{15,000,000 + 2,000,000}$$

$$= 0.1470588 \text{ or } 14.71\%$$

Rate of Return is equivalent to Capitalization Rate. Total Capital Invested is equivalent to Value of the business. Net Operating Income is equivalent to Profit in this example

DISCOUNTED EARNINGS

This determines the value of a small business based upon the present value of projected future earnings, discounted by the required rate of return (capitalization rate). Usually, the question is how well earnings are projected.

XIV. Discounted Cash Flow Valuation Methods

Are the small business valuation methods best used to conduct a business valuation on an entity established for the purpose of fulfilling a specific project, in certain startup and other companies where cash flow is more important than net income, and when a certain time frame is set where an investor wishes to see his investment returned over a specific period of time. In discounted cash flow, the present value of liabilities is subtracted from the combined present value of cash flow and tangible assets, which determines the value of the business.

XV. Price Earnings Multiple

The price-earnings ratio (P/E) is simply the price of a company's share of common stock in the public market divided by its earnings per share. Multiply this multiple by the net income and you will have a value for the business. If the business has no income, there is no business valuation. If the common stock is not publicly traded, business valuation of the stock is purely subjective. This may not be the best choice of business valuation methods, but can provide a benchmark business valuation.

XVI. Dividend Capitalization

Since most closely held companies do not pay dividends, when using dividend capitalization valuators must first determine dividend paying capacity of a business. Dividend paying capacity based on average net income and on average cash flow is used. To determine dividend paying capacity, near term capital needs, expansion plans, debt repayment, operation cushion, contractual requirements, past dividend paying history of a business and dividends of a comparable company should be investigated. After analyzing these factors, percent of average net income and of average cash flow that can be used for the payment of dividends can be estimated. What also must be determined is the dividend yield, which can best be determined by analyzing comparable companies. As with the price earnings ratio method, this usually produces a subjective result.

XVII. Sales Multiple Small Business Valuation Methods

Sales and profit multiples are the most widely used business valuation methods benchmark used in valuing a business. The information needed is annual sales and an industry multiplier, which is usually a range of .25 to 1 or higher. The industry multiplier can be found in various financial publications, as well as analyzing sales of comparable businesses. This method is easy to understand and use. The sales multiple is often used as the business valuation benchmark.

XVIII. Profit Multiple Small Business Valuation

Profit and sales multiples are the most widely used small business valuation benchmarks used in valuing a business. The information needed is pretax profits and a market multiplier, which may be 1, 2, 3, or 4 and usually a ceiling of 5. The market multiplier can be found in various financial publications, as well as analyzing the sale of comparable businesses. These small business valuation methods are easy to understand and use. The profit multiple is often used as the small business valuation ceiling benchmark.

XIX. Liquidation Value

This type of small business valuation is similar to an adjusted book value analysis. Liquidation value is different than a book valuation in that it uses the value of the assets at liquidation, which is often less than market and sometimes book. Liabilities are deducted from the liquidation value of the assets to determine the liquidation value of the small business. Liquidation value can be used to determine the bare bottom benchmark value of a business, since this should be the funds the business may bring upon small business valuation.

XX. Replacement Value

This type of small business valuation is similar to an adjusted book value analysis. Replacement value is different than liquidation value in that is uses the value of the replacement value of assets, which is usually higher than a book valuation. Liabilities are deducted from the replacement value of the assets to determine the replacement value of the small business.

XXI. True Value Small Business Valuation

This is the amount a buyer is finally willing to pay.

Five Business Valuation Myths - By Dr. Stanley J. Feldman

1. Valuing a private business should only be done when the business is ready to be sold or a lender requires a valuation as part of its due diligence process.

If the business is to have a life beyond that of its current owners, then effective planning for ownership transition requires a regular valuation of the business.

2. Businesses in my industry always sell for two times annual revenue (the revenue multiple). So why should I pay someone to value my business?

These rules of thumb used by business brokers, the individuals who often facilitate private business transactions, are median multiple values. The median value indicates that half of the revenue multiples are below the median value and half are above. Thus, the median value is just a convenient midpoint and does not represent the revenue multiple for any actual transaction.

3. A local competitor sold his business for three times revenue six months ago. My business is worth at least this much!

What your business is worth today depends on three factors: 1) how much cash it generates today; 2) expected growth in cash in the foreseeable future; and 3) the return buyers require on their investment in your business.

4. How much a business is worth depends on what the valuation is used for!

There is understandably a wide range of valuation uses. This could be abused to get along on a favorable value of which this should be the case.

5. Your business loses money, so it is not worth much.

Most private businesses appear to lose money. Appearances, however, are often misleading. In the final analysis, there are many important reasons that business owners should know the value of their businesses long before they decided to sell. By understanding the basics outlined above, you should be able to successfully

XXII. Enterprise Value Applications

Enterprise value is more comprehensive than market capitalization, which only reflects common equity. Importantly, EV reflects the opportunistic nature of business and may change substantially over time because of both external and internal conditions. Therefore, financial analysts often use a comfortable range of EV in their calculations.

XXIII. Value Opinion

A real estate broker *opinion of value* is a good source for data gathering. Typically, involve or network this licensed practitioner for inspection of the subject property and recent listings and sales in area of the subject property.

XXIV. Problems Solving

DISCOUNTED CASH FLOW

Example 3 – Estimate the discounted cash flow value of a business that generates a single cash flow of P15,000,000 in 7 years, using a discount rate of 10 percent

$$\text{DISCOUNTED CASH FLOW} = \frac{P15,000,000}{(1 + 10)^7} = P7,697,439$$

Example 4 – Estimate the discounted cash flow value of a business that generates the following cash flows, using a discount rate of 12 percent

Year 1   Cash Flow   14M

Year 2   Cash Flow   18M

Year 3   Cash Flow   24M

Year 4   Cash Flow   87M

Discounted Cash Flow

$$DCF = \frac{14M}{(1+12)^1} + \frac{18M}{(1+12)^2} + \frac{24M}{(1+12)^3} + \frac{87M}{(1+12)^4} = \$99,222,276$$

Discount factor

Year 1 – 0.892857 – 12,499,998

Year 2 – 0.797194 – 14,349,492

Year 3 – 0.711780 – 17,082,720

Year 4 – 0.635518 – 55,290,066

Example 5 – Estimate the discounted cash flow value of a business that generates the following cash flows in four years, using a discount rate of 17 percent

Year 1   Cash Flow - 3M

Year 2   Cash Flow - 11M

Year 3   Cash Flow 270M

$$DCF = \frac{-3M}{(1 + 17)^1} + \frac{-11M}{(1 + 17)^2} + \frac{270M}{(1 + 17)^3} = 157,980,292$$

Discount factor

Year 1 – 0.854700 – -2,564,100

Year 2 – 0.730513 – -8,035,643

Year 3 – 0.624371 – 168,580,035

Example 6 – A firm is expected to earn P7 million in net income in the coming year. Estimate the value of the business, using the information below on similar companies

Company A expected earnings 3M   Value 25 value earnings = 12

Company B expected earnings 5M   Value 48 value earnings = 14

Company C expected earnings 9M   Value 119 value earnings = 16

We first calculate the ratio of value to expected earnings for the similar companies.

The average of these value multiples = 12 + 14 + 16 = 14

We then multiply this average by the firm's expected earnings of 7M by the average of these value multiples = P98,000,000

Example 7 – A firm expects revenues of 36M in the coming year. Estimate the value of the business, using the information below on similar companies

Company A   expected revenues 17   expected earnings 2.9   value 40

Company B   expected revenues 56   expected earnings 8.1   value 186

Company C   expected revenues 29   expected earnings 4.5   value 123

Company D   expected revenues 97   expected earnings 12.7   value 200

Since we are given the revenue number for the firm, we need to calculate the ratio of value revenues for the similar companies

The average of these value multiples = (2.35 + 3.31 + 4.24 + 2.04)/4 = 2.99

The expected revenues = 36 x 2.99 = 107.64M

Example 8 – A firm has inventory worth 7M, machinery worth 21M, buildings worth 50M and land worth 25M. The company owes 15M to suppliers and 45M million in bank. Estimate the liquidation value of the business.

The liquidation value of the business is the value of the assets minus the the liabilities:

$$LIQUIDATION\ VALUE = ASSETS - LIABILITIES$$

$$= 7M + 21 + 75 - (15 + 45) = 43M$$

XXV - Business valuation process

https://accountingweekly.com/steps-in-the-business-valuation-process/

a). Valuation date

b). Going Concern

c). Business Operation

d). Productive assets

e). Historical Position and Performance

f). Normalization of earnings

g). Future Earnings Pattern and volatility

h). Future Earnings Period

i). Forecast Sustainable Earnings

j). Forecast cash flows and free cash flows

k). Business Risk

l). Cost of equity (Cost of Risk) calculation

hapter Seven

XXVI. Assessment

The Real Estate Appraisal and business valuation Investment Tools chapter is with arrays of chapter summary templates that are similar in many ways.

To the students, professionals, bankers, lenders and investors: Should something hamper our decision on basic of business valuation as an investment tools. Let us just visit our undertakings in this chapter:

Again, mathematics as well as appraisal always comes an easy connectivity to other economics and finance sciences. In business formulation and decision makings, appraisal is the main thing so powerful process for personal and business plans. The process of setting goals helps you choose where you want to go in life and in your new business venture. By knowing precisely what you want to achieve, you know where you will have to concentrate your efforts. You'll also quickly spot the distractions that would otherwise lure you from your course. The sequence of getting into the core of business valuation is through the use of different working knowledge of investment tools.

Here we discuss on:

- Business Valuation Organizations

- Business valuation definition

- Business valuation uses

- Reasons for selling

- Potential clients

- Buyers motivation

- Book value

- The formula

- Income capitalization method

- Problem solving

- Discounted cash flow valuation methods

- Price earnings multiple

- Dividend capitalization

- Sales multiple small business valuation methods

- Profit Multiple Small Business Valuation

- Liquidation Value

- Replacement Value

- True Value Small Business Valuation

- Enterprise Value Application

- Value Opinion

- Problem solving

HAPTER EIGHT

BUSINESS ETIQUETTE
OR PROTOCOL

"Manner is personality—the outward manifestation of one's innate character and attitude toward life."

"Manners are like primary colors, there are certain rules and once you have these you merely mix, i.e., adapt, them to meet changing situations."

"Any child can be taught to be beautifully behaved with no effort greater than quiet patience and perseverance, whereas to break bad habits once they are acquired is a Herculean task." - **Emily Post**

I. OBJECTIVE, PURPOSE AND APPROACH

- ➢ To create an awareness why good manners are so important

- ➢ To continuously assist consultants for the industry growth

- ➢ To introduce and communicate basic etiquettes amongst stakeholders

- ➢ To define and instill a sense of self-confidence and poise on a negotiation stage

➤ To provide and understand the framework of a comfortable communication, considerate, and respectful dialogues with others

➤ To Improve or optimize good relationship on all participants

➤ To enhance the fundamental differences between messengers and messages

➤ To develop a knack for business intricacies to a positive direction

After this chapter, you will have learned:

❖ You will know the basic concept of consultancy communication, interaction and result-driven orientation

❖ To promote the ethical development of real estate consultancy in the Philippines.

❖ To continuously assist the growth of the real estate industry

❖ To communicate with developers, practitioners and educators about the importance of business ethics, proper manners and negotiation protocol.

❖ To establish an environment conducive for study and learning.

❖ To introduce the life skills necessary to be successful in quality services

II. The essentials

What are the essentials of getting ahead, albeit good manners?

Established proper etiquette can help people land jobs, get promotions and excel in the relationships with others.

The exemplified successful businessmen and women know how to turn on the charm and exhibit their best business etiquette to get the job done professionally and effectively.

Again, good communication is the genesis and spring board to closing a business deal. For people to get along, work in unison and establish professional relationships with one another, they must communicate with the appropriate etiquette.

Listening skills - the main part of communication etiquette. When others are speaking do not interrupt them. Employ active listening techniques, such as making good eye contact and showing the speaker that you are paying attention to them.

Meeting – Attire - *In advance, what is the reason for the scheduled meeting? What is its agenda, and who made the arrangement? Let us get into the point of view, you as a consultant:*

1). A consultant – getting hired for a particular business consulting

2). The consultant – negotiating representing a client

3). The arrangement and processes involving the limiting parameters on what a consultant can do.

The way you dress impacts whether you have good business etiquette. The business world is professional, and the people who work in it must dress to reflect that level of professionalism. As such, make sure your clothes are clean and pressed, and that you wear suits, blouses, skirts, blazers, ties or other clothing that makes a good impression.

III. Consulting ethical accuracy

a). *Politeness*

To be pleasing, in every opportunity, say **please** and as a gesture of being thankful, do not forget to, say **thank you** in a meeting and more so over a written correspondence. Politeness connotes respect

b). *Best Behavior*

Put your cell phone away during a meeting, and do not engage in side conversations unless you request and granted or allowed as a protocol

c). *Handshake*

Shaking hands with your business counterparts establishes rapport and is in good form. For international interactions, research how that culture greets one another professionally in business, as not all countries see shaking hands as a form of respect.

d). *Table Manners*

Allow the host to make the sitting arrangement

Do not talk when your mouth is full.

No bags or any briefcases on the table

e). *Diplomacy*

Be diplomatic always when engaged in a business conversation, even if you disagree with what others are saying. Apologize if you come to disagree, but do not be afraid to hold true to your convictions.

f). Tone

Never raise your voice to others in the work environment, or use foul language toward them. Keep your tone as neutral as possible.

g). Following Up

As a proper gesture, after a meeting, it is in good form to send a thank-you email or note, recognizing their business or efforts.

IV. Attitude Fit - Habit Learn

1. Standing only!

Stand when meeting someone and/or shaking hands. Do not remain seated while being introduced and/or shaking hands. Show utmost respect, and above all, as much as possible, be an interesting conversationalist. Anything less is, well, just disrespectful.

2. Call Back

return phone calls promptly. It's good business etiquette, and besides, it's something that your competitor may not even be doing! Come with class of distinction and professionalism.

3. You Are Right!

The big game is what is right done by your client, and not what has wrongly gone by. When something is gone wrong on the client's system of doing business, then time it to explore what and how to strategize solution.

4. Use a spell check

The pinnacle of rudeness is not caring enough to take the time to make your communications clear and correct. It is important that you not use shorthand or texting acronyms in business correspondence, by all means, spell your words correctly.

5. Name recall

You stand out. When you remember the names of those you do business with even when on introduction stage.

a) Listen - To what's the name?

b) Repeat - Right back and use them throughout your conversation.

c) Association - helps you to repeat back names in a group in time, place and subject for that meeting

6. Reciprocate with Others

Reciprocate with others who take the time to connect with you. Social media provides unprecedented access to colleagues in your field. Why take the time and energy to invest in a relationship where there's no reciprocity?

7. See through Manners

Follow Up appropriately -- it is good manners. If you promise info, deliver it; if you are asked for something, provide it; if you are given a deadline, meet it. Most importantly, if you want business from someone, remind them periodically of your existence; don't expect them to remember you from one conversation or trade show meeting. In my marketing research, the most frequent tip I hear from government and corporate purchasers is that vendors should follow up better.

8. Cell Phone Etiquette

In today's information age, managing emails, text messages, and phone calls takes considerable time. During business meetings, whether at your office, the office of a client, or even lunch, it is important to recognize that answering phone calls, checking emails, or sending text messages can be very disruptive to the meeting and conveys a message to the participants that they are less important than the party on the phone. Cell phones should be turned off and be out of sight during meetings.

9. Big Etiquette Positive

The biggest etiquette pro that you can do is honor your commitments. When people know you will do what you say, stand behind your word and honor your efforts to them, you will always be successful. Some people fold when times get tough or they're challenged. When people trust you, you are always a leader.

a) Know your prospect and build rapport

b) Be highly intentional and build value

c) Make specific requests

d) Respectfully overcome objections and

e) Gently secure an agreement. When you know who you're talking to, these steps are tasteful with low pressure, yet they're very powerful.

10. Salutation

Good manners and good grammar spell good business.

Use "Dear," "Hi," or "Hello" as a salutation,

11. Watch the Clock

Watch the clock... Be on time. End meetings on time. Never use more words when you could use less.

12. An Invitation That Gets a Yes

The etiquette rule for inviting someone to lunch is the same as for a high school date. If you are the person inviting,

  a) you say why

  b) you say where

  c) you say when.

Meaning to be humble, people say

  a) "We should go to lunch sometime.",

  b) "I'll let you choose where." and

  c) "What's good for you?"

This puts a task (choosing) on the other person's list. Not your prerogative.

Example: "Are you available for lunch at Mosaic next Thursday, noon?" results in a profitable "Yes, thank you."

13. Don't Be a Mailing List Abuser

When you attend a business or social function and exchange business cards with someone, please know that this exchange does not give you the right to add that person to your mailing list. Please be courteous; if you have further contact with this person, either ask their permission to sign them up to your list or ask them to sign up on their own (provide a link). You want your mailing to consist of people who have opted in - you'll get a much higher open rate and more good will as well.

14. Attitude is everything

Etiquette is about rules, and rules are often hard to remember. Business etiquette is no different. The most vital tip is in all you do, remember The Golden Rule. "Treat others the way you want to be treated." This means that it's not about you, it's about them. This must drive your communication, your efforts and interactions. This unique approach stands out in a business world that is largely rude, crude and indifferent.

15. "The Interrupter" Are You One?

One of the worst etiquette no-no's are people who interrupt others either in a business conversation or a presentation.

16. Punctuality, Show Up or Call

A few years ago, I was having difficulty filling a position. I heard that an area professional was interested. After reviewing their qualifications and experience, I confirmed an interview for the next week. Imagine my surprise when the candidate never showed up for the interview or never called.

17. Never Disqualify by Appearance

I've made the mistake of assuming a prospective customer was unable to afford what I was selling based on their appearance. I soon learned that dirty pants and boots, and a soiled ball cap actually meant that this guy owned his own farm and had plenty of money to afford what I was selling in my store. I also learned that the guy with the sharp looking suit and big car was all appearance and no money. Now I treat everyone equally, as it should be.

18. Personalization is Important!

I absolutely hate when people send me a connection request without a personal message. There is too much spam to just send a generic message that offers no insight into why you want to connect. To really harness the power of social media, you need to create real relationships and actually network. Whenever I send out a connection request, I explain why I want to connect so that person knows I am not sending them spam.

19. Never Get Too Busy to....

As a small business owner and F9 Corporate Founder, I always make the time to build and nurture relationships. We tend to meet and work with many people and the difference maker is when we make the effort to build a relationship beyond earning an income. An email, phone call, card, business reference, lunch or a similar interest are all small things any entrepreneur can do with limited time. Business opportunities have come about because of this and it's a great image builder.

20. Write the Right Emails

In this day of email correspondence, it's easy to become too informal. Use of acronyms is rude and unprofessional; therefore learn to write a strong, appropriate business letter the old fashioned way, and use it in your email. Be sure to address the person by the correct title, and by all means, spell their name right! Proofread it at least three times before you send it and have another pair of eyes review it, too. You'll be rewarded with a great, professional first impression!

21. Stand Out with Simplicity

The one biggest etiquette "do" that I implement daily and has led to client confidence and referrals is responding in a timely fashion, even with a minor detail or update. It goes a long way in establishing or maintaining relationships. When clients email, I (usually) respond within minutes. It's amazing how this simple tip sets me apart from so many other businesses that "get to it when they get to it." The time invested is minutes, but the value is truly forever.

22. Mind the Time, Shirt, & Talk!

Be on time, or be 5 minutes early if possible. No one likes to wait or listen to stupid excuses... Appreciate others' time & schedule by being on time & finishing on time.

Dress up! Yes, you're an entrepreneur & you can dress the way you want, but it's not OK to show up for a meeting in a Hawaiian shirt, shorts or sandals!

Don't give your sales pitch as if you're throwing up, i.e. loud, in one breath, and ends with an "aah I'm done" kind of expression... Breathe, ask questions, & let others talk too...

23. Put Your Cell Phone Away

Do not place your telephone on the table during a meeting. Best option - leave your cell phone in the car or in your briefcase. Having it in front of you is a distraction to both you and your client and it sends a negative message that you don't mind interrupting your meeting for something inconsequential. Schedule a time to return all phone messages on the same business day.

24. Don't Turn Your Back

I complimented a fence builder in my neighborhood and asked him for his business card. He told me he didn't have a card and turned his back on me. I walked away thinking he just lost a very strong potential customer.

Tip: When asked for a business card, stop what you're doing, greet the person asking and show interest in him or her. Never turn your back on the prospective customer. If you don't have a business card, explain that you ran out, ask for her card and follow up later!

25. The Power of the Written Word!

Do not underestimate the importance of the written word. A poorly written message will have a major impact on your business. It is imperative to proofread for: Spelling- Spell-check will not correct your use of their vs. there; Grammar- 90% of the time, you can correct your own mistakes. Most errors are due to hasty writing; Tone- The most important part of writing is the tone. If the tone of the message is wrong, the message will be lost on the reader. Please proofread your work and write well!

26. Send Handwritten Thank Yous

Creating a great business is about building and maintaining positive relationships. Everyone appreciates being acknowledged for their gift of money and time. So, send handwritten "Thank you" notes. No time? If you want to be successful, you need to find the time. Always carry "thank you" note cards already stamped. Write when you have a few moments, i.e. at the airport. Expense? You need nothing fancy. A simple card and a stamp will do. Poor penmanship? Write slower. Stand out! Send a handwritten Thank you!

a). Must express my appreciation

b). So be grateful for your contribution

c). Unequal in effort

d). Done with such expertise

e). An exemplary performance

f). Offer my sincerest appreciation

g). I was so impress by

h). Your performance is noteworthy

i). Set an outstanding example for

j). Demonstrate such dedication

27. Watch Where You Say it!

Communication skills can carry you to the top or the bottom. A man was on the elevator with a friend criticizing the intelligence of the CEO. The CEO's daughter was on the elevator.

It may help you to complain about a person, but choose an appropriate location. If you trust the person you are venting to, your comments may still get back to the person. VENT to yourself. Go for a walk and vent. So what if others think you are crazy for talking to yourself; you will still have your job.

28. Busy, Busy, Busy

Everyone is busy. When you are late, the other person feels devalued. If this happens, you need to call and be responsible for your actions. Don't make excuses, just be straight. "I am running 10 minutes late." No one likes to wait. Being late says, my time is more important than yours. They may not be happy with the call, but it will be more acceptable than just showing up late. It will show that you value them and business is all about building relationships.

29. Try Not to Appear Desperate

Business is abuzz with the notion of authenticity, but disclosure to the point of desperation does not bode well. Over the course of a conversation with an event planner I was looking to hire, she revealed, "To be honest, we would do anything to be associated with your firm. And we really need the work!"

30. Store the Shades

Even if the future looks bright, please avoid wearing sunglasses on your head or face during a business meeting. This may be trendy in the Sun Belt for long weekends, but in the world of business, it can be construed as unprofessional. Worse, you could be viewed as untrustworthy in certain industries and cultures. Exceptions: if you're a professional poker player, troubled celebrity, reviewing a record deal with a top producer, or will be participating in an outdoor sporting event with clients.

31. Common Courtesy: Lost?

We're in dire need of correction in society and it's time to go "back to basics" with common courtesy. An annoyance of late seems to occur within business lunches, when I have that all important one on one time with a business associate or client. It goes without saying that cell phone usage is just plain rude, but even more so, is when an acquaintance of my guest stops by the table, and no introduction nor an acknowledgment of my presence is made. Little do they know, but this is a deal breaker!

32. Don't Get Too Relaxed

At business lunches, dinners, and networking events, it is possible to be too relaxed. Watch the alcohol intake. We've all seen the tipsy employee who's making an impression, but not the impression they intended. The same goes for the person who accompanies the employee to the event. Their inappropriate behavior will be remembered. "Remember the guy Sally brought to the picnic last year?" Mum was right. We're judged by the company we keep. Any event that is connected to work is still work.

33. Always Show Appreciation

Remember to thank those who refer you business. Small business people are busy, and showing appreciation is often viewed as a second tier priority. But the little things matter. Forget a "thank you" and miss out on repeat referrals. Have a way of thanking people built in as a procedure. One idea is that you can create a field in your client database that does not let you create an invoice for a new client until a thank you is sent to the referral source.

34. An Unprofitable Mix

Beliefs, whether political, social or religious, are best not merged with your business marketing, including social media. Although I consider myself a person with strong religious convictions, I resent having a marketer's convictions in the arena with their brand, product or service. It often seems fake and pretentious and results in devaluing, not only the brand, but also the business individuals' belief itself. Let your ideals show in your actions and practices, not your marketing.

35. Profit potentials, benefit and Punctuality

Punctuality is a must! Be on time for every appointment. Always finish the job ahead of time. Those are two of the best ways to get people to help you in your business and to get repeat business. "Half of success is just showing up in a timely manner."

Role play

Phone scenario 1 – When you pick up a phone – as **receiver**

1. Greet the caller

2. Identify you company,

3. identify yourself,

4. ask what you can do for the caller

   Example "Good morning, this is F9 Management and Consultancy, Joy here, how may I help you?"

Phone scenario 2 – When you dial the phone – **as caller**

The caller then has an opportunity to greet you and state the purpose of the call.

Example "Hello Joy, this is Carol from the University Academic Department, do you have a minute to talk about the latest management trend where you are in the business now?"

Phone scenario 3 – Joy as receiver

Assertive yet polite because she cannot entertain further on this unsolicited intrusion to her time … she remains courteous. She answers her. No Carol, I am afraid I'm busy at the moment preparing for conference. Could you call back at the same time tomorrow?

Phone scenario 4 – Carol as caller

Intrusive acknowledges and confirming to call again the following day. Then the final greetings follow: Certainly, Joy, I'll call you tomorrow morning at 10 a.m. Good bye

Phone Scenario 5 – Joy the receiver returns the greetings to Carol the caller.

Final phone scenario 6 – the receiver waits the caller to settle the phone set before she does hers.

Phrases for an effective "building block" from *How to write it*

by Sandra E. Lamb

    a). Must express my appreciation

    b). So grateful for your contribution

    c). Unequaled effort

    d). Done with such expertise

e). An exemplary performance

f). Offer my sincerest appreciation

g). I was so impressed by

h). Your performance is noteworthy

i). Set an outstanding example for

j). Demonstrate such dedication

hapter EIGHT

V. Assessment

Let us visit our undertakings in this chapter:

Here we study, discuss and evaluate on:

- Real Estate Consultant ethical standard

- Consultant – client interaction

- Behavior - Attitude

- Appointment - Meeting

- Environmental Concerns

1. APPROACHES TO BUSINESS ETHICS

When business people speak about "business ethics" they usually mean one of three things:

a). avoid breaking the criminal law in one's work-related activity;

b). avoid action that may result in civil law suits against the company; and

c). avoid actions that are bad for the company image. Businesses are especially concerned with these three things since they involve loss of money and company reputation.

2. DOING BUSINESS IN FOREIGN COUNTRIES

The moral challenge for businesses here in the United States it difficult enough when balancing one's profit interests against the needs of employees, consumers, governments and special interest groups.

The moral challenge is even more intense for multinational companies who need to live up to moral expectations both in the US and in host foreign countries. In developed countries, the moral expectations of the host country are as stringent as our own. With third world host countries, though, the moral expectations often more lax, and multinationals are tempted to lower their standards when situations permit. In this chapter we will look at three areas of moral concern for multinationals: bribery, influencing foreign governments, and exploiting third world countries.

3. BUSINESS AND THE ENVIRONMENT

The greatest damage done to the environment is inflicted by business and industry, and not from domestic activities. Businesses extract the greatest tolls in terms of energy consumption, toxic waste, air and water pollution, and deforestation. Increasing amounts of industrial toxic waste contaminates ground water, which in turn becomes harmful for human consumption. Oil spills from petroleum industries destroy shorelines and kill millions of sea animals. The burning of fossil fuels such as oil, gas and coal produces excess carbon dioxide, which adds to global warming through a greenhouse effect. Fluorocarbon gasses used in making domestic products such as refrigerators and styrofoam depletes the earth's ozone layer, which shields the earth from the sun's life-destroying ultraviolet rays. Some of these problems are expensive nuisances, such as oil spills and toxic waste. Others, though, threaten the survival of life on our planet, such as carbon dioxide production and the release of fluorocarbon gasses. In this chapter we will look at some of the causes of environmental irresponsibility in businesses, and some theories about why businesses should be more responsible.

Code of Ethics: A company's Code of Ethics contains the ethical standards to which it commits itself and its employees.

Values usually are both ethical and operational in nature in the workplace.

A ***Code of Conduct*** is a longer document, which states or summarizes a company's ethics policies or practices. Codes of conduct normally address such issues as privacy of information; use of company resources; use of information technology; travel, entertainment and gifts; conflicts of interest; political contributions; and relationships with suppliers and competitors. A code of conduct illustrates how a company's values translate into concrete policies and procedures.

Compliance: *Compliance* usually refers to an organization's conformance with the laws and regulations relevant to its activities and also may refer to a company's conformance with its *ethical* policies and practices.

Business ethics is the broadest of the three terms. It addresses the morality of both economic systems (e.g., the free market, socialism, communism) and the conduct of the organizations found within these systems (e.g., corporations in a free market system).

Corporate ethics may be viewed as a subset of business ethics. Corporate ethics focuses specifically on issues of morality associated with business enterprises. These include relations internal to the organization (e.g., treatment of employees, dealings with shareholders, questions concerning product quality and customer service, etc.) as well as external relations (e.g., interactions with government, specific communities, society as a whole, the impact of corporate activities on the natural environment, etc.).

Corporate social responsibility, in turn, is a subset of corporate ethics. Its focus is the firm's economic, social, and environmental impact upon the broader community of which it is a part, and the nature of the company's responsibilities to the society in which it participates.

Ethical Values: Core aspirations which are embedded in ethical standards for human conduct. For example, the value of honesty leads to the principle of truth-telling, i.e., the moral obligation to not lie or mislead.

Ethics: Ethics and morality frequently are treated as synonyms in everyday conversation. While these terms are closely related, they are distinct.

Morality is part of practice. Specifically, morality is human action which is aligned with standards of moral obligation or moral value. Thus, an act is said to be moral if it is consistent with judgments about our moral duties (e.g., "keep your promises," "don't lie," etc.), or judgments of moral value (e.g., "always honor human dignity," "support the common good").

Ethics is the study of morality. Ethics critically reflects on such issues as the nature of moral obligation and moral value – that is, on the concepts and understandings which guide decisions about what we should (or should not) do. Ethics seeks to answer such questions as: *What do (or should) we mean by "good" and "bad," or "right" and "wrong"? What actions are we obliged to take or avoid? What traits or habits (virtues) should we develop, to enable us to consistently do the right thing?*

A *stakeholder* is any group or individual who can affect or is affected by an organization's decisions and activities. A company's stakeholders are said to include customers, employees, employees, shareholders, suppliers and communities. An expanded interpretation also might identify as stakeholders such groups as financiers, competitors, unions, the media, government, political organizations, and activist groups.

HAPTER NINE

REAL ESTATE CONSULTANCY

Education is the most powerful weapon which you can use to change the world. I learned that courage was not the absence of fear, but the triumph over it. The brave man is not he who does not feel afraid, but he who conquers that fear. - **Nelson Mandela. A Nobel Prize Winner who retired from retirement and passed away at the age of 95.**

I. OBJECTIVE, PURPOSE AND APPROACH

➢ To promote the development of real estate consultancy in the Philippines.

➢ To continuously assist the growth of the real estate industry

➢ To communicate with developers, practitioners and educators about the importance of business valuation, real estate appraisal, consultancy and environmental educations.

➢ To define the needs and methodologies in the system, observing the position of the client and their requirements, and the project goals.

➢ To understand the current process in the collection of relevant data.

➢ To improve or optimize the current process based upon data analysis using innovative techniques

➢ To know the fundamental differences between real estate appraisal, business valuation, feasibility study and consultancy

➢ To develop a knack for business intricacies and develop it to a positive direction

➢ To correlate the advantages and disadvantages of valuation and appraisal methods for consultancy engagement

➢ To establish an environment conducive for study and learning.

➢ To allow the opportunity to identify on time and effort spent

➢ To introduce the life skills necessary to be successful in quality services

PROJECT FEASIBILITY STUDY PREPARATION

1. **PROJECT CONCEPT**
2. PRE FEASIBILITY
3. **PROPER FEASIBILITY**
4. **DETAILED ENGINEERING**
5. **CONSTRUCTION DEVELOPMENT**
6. **OPERATION MAINTENANCE**
7. POST FEASIBILITY

After this chapter, you will have learned:

❖ You will know the basic concept of real estate consultancy for an interesting and understanding problems solving as an critical tools thorough analysis,

❖ How to present to business clients different financial comparative approaches to make

❖ How to knowledgeably sell, persuade and convince your clients on the service or product you present.

II. Real Estate Consultant

Real Estate Consulting means – making better decisions for a client for a fee. He assists turning critical and complex issues into opportunities for growth for business owners and investors to lenders and corporate groups. He offers you the experience, know-how, and the strategic planning that helps lead to better decisions through due diligence, market studies, portfolio services, lease advisory, and more with all others you need to enhance the value of a client's business.

The true real estate consultant will get paid for all their work. These knowledgeable and savvy Investors or developers shall embrace a method to save transaction costs and increase their business profitability.

This compensation is up-front, as agreed upon in the term of reference.

III. History of Consultancy

Who is a real estate Consultant? – He is a licensed real estate broker with at least ten years of registered practice in the Philippines or with a five years registered practice as a licensed real estate appraiser to qualify for Professional Regulation Commission examination given on a December each year for a written exam followed by an oral exam before of **PRBRES** commissioners. The Professional Regulation Commission maiden exam given was in 2011 topped by **Atty Leni Go** with **Engr Nono Catolico** coming in as second place. I am so proud to heed their request having me solely as their seminar-lecturer. In return they gifted me with a 100% passing (inclusive: **Cristy Lugtu**, **Dal Gambe** and **Gigi Roa**).

PRC 2011 – Topnothers-all and 100% passing

CONGRATULATIONS
TO YOU WHO IS TO TAKE THE FIRST BOLD STEP

1. Marjorie Bandolon Cartojano of the Philippines-Diliman	University **81.90**
2. Rey Dungog Cartojano of the Philippines-Diliman	University **81.70**
3. Allan Du Yaphockun of San Carlos	University **80.70**

PRC Real Estate Consultant 2012 – Top notchers both

It is noteworthy to reminisced that the following year, again the number one in the consultant board was no other than Economist-Consultant **Maya Bandolon-Cartojano**, followed closely, but not quite closed, to no other than 2018 PAREB President **Atty Rey Cartojano**. It is an honor to get beat by the "better half", all told. Again it is noteworthy to know that on the first exam given we were striving to be within the first 50 consultant-licensees in the country. By 2017 year -end we are only within the striking number of 200 licensees produced in the country.

So, we can imagine, spread our consultants on the 18 regions in the Philippines: with 82 provinces, 134 highly urbanized, independent and component cities. In effect, our profession is highly in demand. We are way off in the theory of equilibrium to supply the real estate consultancy market. Simply put, the industry does not know that well that our breed exist. Unless we reach out to them - we must enhance our practice and let them know - that is marketing our services in the highest order. By now, the industry has already produced some two hundred licensed consultants over the span of seven years, and more or less some overall we have a supposedly two hundred fifty warm and true blooded real estate consultant practicing professionals.

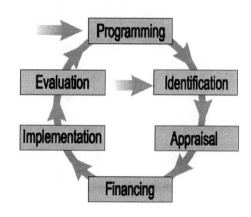

Investment and Feasibility Analysis- Feasibility analysis is undertaken for new projects, rehabilitation projects, and modernization projects and seeks to answer the questions

How is the project feasible? Or the project must be:

> a). Legally permissible

> b). Physically possible

> c). Environmentally friendly

> d). Financially viable

> e). Technically manageable

> f). Socially Acceptable

> g). Economically profitable

> h) Culturally reasonable

PROJECT FEASIBILITY CYCLE

IV. Consultant's expertise on PFS Preparation

    a). Pre-project feasibility study – As a concept, first step before proceeding

    b). Project feasibility study proper

    c). Post feasibility study – At this stage, answers to queries must have had made available

V. How do we become a real estate consultant?

This is the norm and form as standard practice in the PRC licensure examination:

1. Pre-qualify to take test

2. Take a 120 lecture hours from an accredited provider.

3. Prepare a project feasibility study to present before a PRBRES panel

4. Pass the written licensure exam

5. Pass the oral licensure and PFS presentation examination

6. Register and obtain the license from Professional Regulation Commission.

7. Do the consulting practice

VI. What consultant services can be offered to the industry?

1. Business plan preparation and consulting

2. Real estate consulting

3. Feasibility study preparation

4. Project implementation

5. Enterprise Management

VII. How is consultant get paid

What is the meaning of property consultant? The Real Estate Consultant is the link between defining the problem and devising a solution of measurable economic value. It is a broad based role, within which there are specialist operators providing advice.

Consulting is about offering quality, transparent choices, both in the types of services that you can receive and how those services can be paid for. The Real Estate Consultant is compensated for their expertise, time and/or the task.

VIII. Some comparative practices:

SALESPERON	BROKER	APPRAISER	CONSULTANT
Works through a Broker	Works for a firm or do the business Independently.	Works independently	Works independently for a fee as agreed and may be for a profit share
Sell for Commission	Sell for a	Fee as agreed and not on a contingent basis from an assignment result	
Services for a professional fee	Fee or Commission		As a generalist As a specialist

Mandate - Accreditation	Mandate – Licensure	Mandate Licensure exam	Mandate Licensure exam
Academic need 2-year college study	Academic need BSREM	Academic need BSREM	Academic need 10 years as Broker or 5 years as Appraiser

Comparative

USA Practice

Salesperson	Broker	Appraiser	Consultant
By licensure exam	Licensure exam	4-categories of Licensure exam 1. Temp License 2. License 3. Certified 4. General	No licensure exam

IX. Consultancy Tools – (1)

Porter's Five Forces

Company's Competitive Forces to Maximize Profitability

This is a simple but powerful tool for understanding the competitiveness of your business environment, and for identifying your strategy's potential profitability.

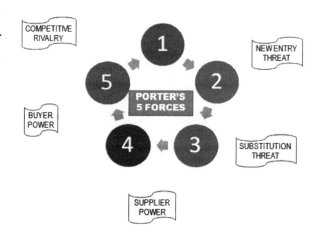

Here we can understand the forces in your environment or industry that affects business profitability; we'll be able to adjust strategy accordingly.

For example, you could take fair advantage of a strong position or improve a weak one, and avoid taking wrong steps in the future.

Again, the basics of **SMART** comes into the center stage of consultancy.

1. **Competitive Rivalry.** Would you know at the specialization and strength of your industry players? How many rivals do you have? Who are they, and how does the quality of their products and services compare with yours?

Where rivalry is intense, companies can attract customers with aggressive price cuts and high-impact marketing campaigns. Also, in markets with lots of rivals, your suppliers and buyers can go elsewhere if they feel that they're not getting a good deal from you.

On the other hand, the theory of supply and demand, where competitive rivalry is minimal, and no one else is doing what you do, then you'll likely have tremendous strength and healthy profits.

2. **Supplier Power.** On the knowledge, determines by how easy it is for your suppliers to increase their prices. How many potential suppliers do you have? How unique is the product or service that they provide, and how expensive would it be to switch from one supplier to another?

The more you have to choose from, the easier it will be to switch to a cheaper alternative. But the fewer suppliers there are, and the more you need their help, the stronger their position and their ability to charge you more. That can impact your profit.

3. **Buyer Power.** Here, you ask yourself how easy it is for buyers to drive your prices down. How many buyers are there, and how big are their orders? How much would it cost them to switch from your products and services to those of a rival? Are your buyers strong enough to dictate terms to you?

When you deal with only a few savvy customers, they have more power, but your power increases if you have many customers.

4. **Threat of Substitution.** This refers to the likelihood of your customers finding a different way of doing what you do. For example, if you supply a unique software product that automates an important process, people may substitute it by doing the process manually or by outsourcing it. A substitution that is easy and cheap to make can weaken your position and threaten your profitability.

5. **Threat of New Entry.** Your position can be affected by people's ability to enter your market. So, think about how easily this could be done. How easy is it to get a

foothold in your industry or market? How much would it cost, and how tightly is your sector regulated?

If it takes little money and effort to enter your market and compete effectively, or if you have little protection for your key technologies, then rivals can quickly enter your market and weaken your position. If you have strong and durable barriers to entry, then you can preserve a favorable position and take fair advantage of it.

X. Consultancy Tools – (2)

Vilfredo Federico Damaso Pareto (Italian: Pareto Principle (also termed the 80-20 rule).

He made several important contributions to economics, particularly in the study of income distribution and in the analysis of individuals' choices. He introduced the concept of Pareto efficiency and helped develop the field of microeconomics. He was also the first to discover that income follows a Pareto distribution, which is a power law probability distribution. The Pareto principle was named after him, and it was built on observations of his such as that 80% of the land in Italy

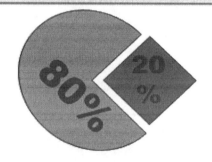

was owned by about 20% of the population. He also contributed to the fields of sociology and mathematics,

> *Likewise, the wealth of a nation, similarly, the Philippines: 80% of the country's wealth is in the hands of the 20% of its people.*

Further, n 1906, Pareto made the famous observation that twenty percent of the population owned eighty percent of the property in Italy.

One of Pareto's equations achieved special prominence, and controversy. He was fascinated by problems of power and wealth. How do people get it? How is it distributed around society? How do those who have it use it? The gulf between rich and poor has always been part of the human condition, but Pareto resolved to measure it. Society was not a "social pyramid" with the proportion of rich to poor sloping gently from one class to the next. Instead it was more of a "social arrow" – very fat on the bottom where the mass of men live, and very thin at the top where sit the wealthy elite. Nor was this effect by chance; the data did not remotely fit a bell curve, as one would expect if wealth were distributed randomly. "It is a social law", he wrote: something "in the nature of man".

How To Apply The 80 20 Rule To Time Management

Here's what you should do in order to effectively apply the 80/20 rule to goal setting and to your overall productivity.

Daily Work –Hours Activities:

Heavy – Heavier – Heaviest

Personal + Routine + Mental + Action + decision

$(20 + 20 + 20 + 20)\% = 80\%$ time spent, $(10 + 10)\%$

= 20% result produced

$(10 + 10)\% = 20\%$ time spent, $(20 + 20 + 20 + 20)\%$

= 80% result produced

*If you could only identify which time of the day is priority to give attention to the heaviest aspect in the list, which one goal would have the greatest positive impact on your **Just in Time((JIT)** attitude to accomplishment.*

You should continue to work at those goals that you've chosen as the most valuable all the time.

A lot of people appear to be busy all day long but seem to accomplish very little. This is almost always because they are busy working on tasks that are of low value while they are procrastinating on the one or two activities that could make a real difference to their companies and to their careers.

The most valuable tasks you can do each day are often the hardest and most complex, but the payoff and rewards for completing them can be tremendous.

Before you begin work, always ask yourself, *"Is this task in the top 20 percent of my activities or in the bottom 80 percent?"*

The rule for this is: resist the temptation to clear up small things first.

If you choose to start your day working on low-value tasks, you will soon develop the habit of always starting and working on low-value tasks.

Always Work Towards Your Main Goal

Finally, I want to tell you about a study that has just been done about the attitudes of rich people versus poor people in regard to goal setting. What they found is that 85% of rich people have one big goal that they work on all the time. So, if you want to be wealthy, do what wealthy people do.

Those are my strategies for applying the 80 20 Rule.

My question today is: *"Do you use the 80 20 Rule for goal setting, and if you do, what changes have you noticed in your life?*

Using The Pareto Rule To Achieve Success In Life

"You must dream big dreams, for only big dreams have the power to move the minds of men." When you begin to dream big dreams, your levels of self-esteem and self-confidence will go up immediately. You will feel more powerful about yourself and your ability to deal with what happens to you. The reason so many people accomplish so little is because they never allow themselves to lean back and imagine the kind of life that is possible for them.

The 80 20 Rule In Action

He applied the 80 20 rule to his client base.

What he found was that 20 percent of his clients contributed 80 percent of his profits. He also found that the amount of time spent on a high-profit client was pretty much the same amount of time spent on a low-profit client.

Identify Your Constraints

The 3 Keys To Living Without Limits

The three keys to living without limits have always been the same. They are clarity, competence, and concentration.

What It Means

The 80/20 Rule means that in any situation, 20 percent of the inputs or activities are responsible for 80 percent of the outcomes or results. In Pareto's case, it meant 20 percent of the people owned 80 percent of the wealth. In Juran's initial work applying the 80/20 rule to quality studies, he identified 20 percent of the defects causing 80 percent of the problems.

Project Managers know that 20 percent of the work (the first 10 percent and the last 10 percent) consume 80 percent of the time and resources.

Other examples you may have encountered:

Example:

- ➢ 80% of our revenues are generated by 20% of our customers.

- ➢ 80% of our complaints come from 20% of our customers.

- ➢ 80% of our quality issues occur with 20% of our products.

- ➢ 20% of our contributors provide 80% of our funding.

- ➢ 20% of our employees are responsible for 80% of sick days.

- ➢ 20% of my ideas generate 80% of my traffic on my blog.

There are a nearly unlimited number of examples that we tend to apply the 80/20 rule to in our personal and working lives. Most of the time, we are referencing Pareto's Rule without applying rigorous mathematical analysis to the situation.

Pareto's Principle or the 80/20 Rule is a useful construct when analyzing our efforts and outcomes. It is priceless when applied to task or goal lists, and it provides a useful analytical framework

XI. Consultancy Tools – (3)

W. Edwards Deming - *It is not enough to do your best; you must know what to do, and then do your best.*

The theory of PDCA

1. **PDCA (plan–do–check–act - Deming** circle/cycle/wheel **or plan–do–check–adjust**

2. **PDSA. (plan–do–study–act) - Shewart circle/cycle/wheel**

3. **OPDCA (observe-plan-do-check-act)** another version of this PDCA

All of the above is an iterative four-step management method used in business for the control and continual improvement of processes and products and of course business and real estate consultancy for a fee.

PLAN

Establish the objectives and processes necessary to deliver results in accordance with the expected output (the target or goals). By establishing output expectations, the completeness and accuracy as part of the targeted improvement. As much as possible start it from small task towards bigger ones.

DO

Implement the plan, execute the process. Collect data for charting and analysis in the following "CHECK" and "ACT" steps.

CHECK

Study the actual results (measured and collected in "DO" above) and compare against the expected results (targets or goals from the "PLAN") to ascertain any differences.

ACT

If the CHECK shows that the PLAN that was implemented in DO is an improvement to the prior standard (baseline), then that becomes the new standard (baseline) for how the organization should ACT going forward to the new standard If the CHECK shows that the PLAN that was implemented in DO is not an improvement, then the existing standard (baseline) will remain in place. In either case, if the CHECK showed something different than expected (whether better or worse), then there is some more learning to be done... and that will suggest potential future PDCA cycles. Note that some who teach PDCA assert that the ACT involves making adjustments or corrective actions... but generally it would be counter to PDCA thinking to propose and decide upon alternative changes without using a proper PLAN phase, or to make them the new standard (baseline) without going through DO and CHECK steps.

XII. Consultancy Tools – (4)

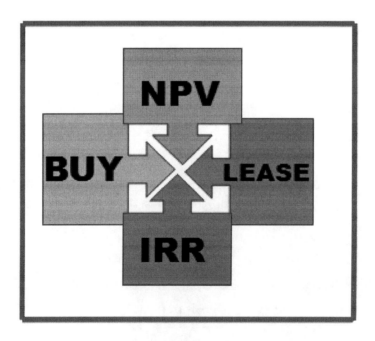

BUY VS LEASE DECISION MAKING – The tools we are to use is the Net present value and Internal Rate of Return

Net present value (NPV) - A method used in evaluating investments, whereby the net present value of all cash outflows (such as the cost of the investment) and cash inflows (returns) is calculated using a given discount rate, usually required rate of return. An investment is acceptable if the NPV is positive, reject if less than one and analyze involving other parameters if equivalent to zero and thereat.

Internal Rate of Return (IRR) - Rate of return that equates the present value of future cash flows to the initial investment. Also referred to as the yield on investments. Interest rate - The rate of interest charged for the use of money, usually expressed as an annual rate. The rate is derived by dividing the amount of interest by the amount of principal borrowed.

Investment - The purchase of real property, stocks, bonds, collectible annuities, mutual fund shares, etc, with the expectation of realizing income or capital gain, or both, in the future. Investment is longer term and usually less risky than speculation.

Lease - A contract where a party being the owner (lessor) of an asset (leased asset) provides the asset for use by the lessee at a consideration (rentals), either fixed or dependent on any variables, for a certain period

XIII. Investment tools

- Financial ratio

- Statistics

- Internal rate of return (IRR)

- Net present Value (NPV)

- Break-even point (BEP)

- Cash Flow

- Cost of capital

- Margin of Safety

- Weighted average cost of capital (WACC)

- Benefit) – Cost (B/C

- Profitability index

- Payback Period

- Inflation

- Gross Domestic Product (GDP)

- Payment Plan

- Lease vs Buy Theory

- Gross Income Multiplier (GIM)

- Supply and Demand

- Depreciation

XIV. Preliminary Meeting

Preliminary meeting - This is an appointment set to discuss of the problem why a business valuation is needed. This is the time the client will ask what are the expected deliverables and here the preliminary benchmark is identified. First, identify why a business valuation is required. Second, what the business consultant can offer as a solution to the situation.

XV. Environmental Concerns

1. Vulnerability

The degree to which a system is susceptible to, or unable to cope with, adverse effects of climate change, including climate variability and extremes. Vulnerability is a function of the character, magnitude, and rate of climate variation to which a system is exposed; its sensitivity; and its adaptive capacity.

2. Climate Change

Climate change refers to any significant change in the measures of climate lasting for an extended period of time. In other words, climate change includes major changes in temperature, precipitation, or wind patterns, among others, that occur over several decades or longer.

3. Abrupt Climate Change

Sudden (on the order of decades), large changes in some major component of the climate system, with rapid, widespread effects.

4. Adaptation

Adjustment or preparation of natural or human systems to a new or changing environment which moderates harm or exploits beneficial opportunities.

5. Adaptive Capacity

The ability of a system to adjust to climate change (including climate variability and extremes) to moderate potential damages, to take advantage of opportunities, or to cope with the consequences.

XVI. Project Feasibility Study Report writing - It's good to note that consultancy project feasibility study report writing is a team work of economic and finance structures, technical, geographic, demographic, urban and regional analysis writing. We, consultants are there to conduct and coordinate the on-going report writing.

hapter Nine

XVII. Assessment

ACADEMIA MAXIMA
(THE 8 P PLAN)-Dr. Tomasito Z. Academia
HOW TO STRATEGIZE ENTERPRISE

PLAN PURPOSELY

PREPARE PRAYERFULLY

PROCEED POSITIVELY

PURSUE PERSISTENTLY

PERSEVERE PAINSTAKINGLY

POTENTIALS & POSSIBILITIES

PRESENT PERSUASIVELY

PROTECT AND PRESERVE

The Real Estate Appraisal and business valuation Investment Tools chapter is with arrays of chapter summary templates that are similar in many ways. To the students, professionals, bankers, lenders and investors: Should something hamper our decision on basic of business valuation as an investment tools. Let us just visit our undertakings in this chapter:

Again, mathematics as well as appraisal always comes an easy connectivity to other economics and finance sciences. In business formulation and decision makings, appraisal is the main thing so powerful process for personal and business plans. The process of setting goals helps you choose where you want to go in life and in your new business venture. By knowing precisely what you want to achieve, you know where you will have to concentrate your efforts. You'll also quickly spot the distractions that would otherwise lure you from your course.

The sequence of getting into the core of business valuation is through the use of different working knowledge of investment tools.

Here we study, discuss and evaluate on:

- Real Estate Consultant

- History of Consultancy

- Consultant's expertise

- How do we become a real estate consultant?

- What consultant services can be offered to the industry?

- How is consultant get paid

- Preliminary Meeting

- Environmental Concerns

SPEECH OF DOCTOMS – February 2018

" AS SPEAKERS, WE EXIST FOR ONE REASON: TO COMMUNICATE LIFE-CHANGING MESSAGES. "

The WISDOM I learned was from a **"no read no write man,"** who was born in 1907. If he is with me today He would be 120 years old. Passed yonder at 93 years old without visiting a hospital, not even once, believe me except, but for an extraction of a tooth ache.

He is **Monico Academia-my grandfather**. He didn't die, he simply fade away with his WISDOM indelibly leaving a legacy in my life, which is a part of what I am today.

"It won't be a problem if you aim high and miss, but it becomes a real issue if you aim low and hit." – his aim in life is on humility, frugality and simplicity. My grandpa says…

Monico with my grandma were blessed with 9 children. They lived in a community in Basilan down south of the Philippines, an island twenty miles off Zamboanga City. In their community, sending a child to passed elementary school is already a feat by itself. Not even 5% of their class graduate high school. But my grandpa's children of nine – all finished and with a college degree. Six of their children are all on their golden ages now, including Dr. Tomasito, my daddy who is 75 years old this year, alive and kicking: plays good chess, tennis and boxing. A super sports buff.

Henry Ford, saying, "If you think you can or if you think you can't, you're right." – my dad, as an academician loves excellence for the love of it but abhors perfectionism.

Their common secret – though they are the poorest in town yet they are the fullest of wisdom, they **take the simplest of food but share the most in life.** His secret is to **simplify your given situation amidst complexities. Seize the opportunities up front.**

An educated person is one who can cope up on any situation in life

Next, let's deal with the man worth of my respect, admiration and emulation. SMART but not the smartest, so ordinary yet doing so extraordinary things in his life. He succeeded upon my MOMMY to have eight kids in the family including their fourth child in me.

My DADDY is smart: in his younger days, as poor as he was, though a college dropout married my mother who is already a physician, rich girl from Mindanao, daughter of a town mayor. My father thought he had it all, yes but only to find out in a quagmire of desires and slipping DIGNITY. His dignity is losing grip in his life.

In the early 70s, he was the family driver of his rich wife.

So after having three children, he went back to college, bit the dust, swallowed his pride and bitter taste the bullet, at long last graduated from college without pomposity and ceremony, was it too late? Not at all only after 12 years, my poor dad barely made it. "Son, you'd rather be an hour early than a minute late in seizing opportunities" Or better still, better late than to have never graduated at all.

Doc Tom Sr. – my poor DAD went to University of the Philippines at the age of 56 and earned his diploma in Urban and Regional planning degree (DURP). The first to have six degree licenses from PRC on this particular courses. My dad is a board top notcher.

He is oldest in the history to pass the license exam for professional teacher (LET) at the age of 71, with two doctorate degrees. He travels all over the country and the world over.

Now, the person in front of you DOC TOM JR - is a national UAAP university league tennis champion. has made travel multiple times compared to my dad. "Son, make sure, you make yourself available as servant for a qualification to leadership." No matter what, you don't give up.", my dad says

On Poor Dad- Rich Son relationship built-up

Doc Tom Sr. becomes rich because of rich son? Rich of what?

Why the difference? We are both planners, again the difference? Tom Sr. doesn't take a risk. Tom Jr. welcomes the risk. The higher the risk the more challenging and merrier it becomes for me. That is Doc Tom Jr. speaking before you now

Ladies and gentlemen: What our aspiration for a better contribution and sharing in life is the reason why we are here today.

Seize the opportunity and tons of opportunities abound all around us

ACADEMIA MAXIMA

(THE 8 P PLAN)-Dr. Tomasito Z. Academia
HOW TO STRATEGIZE ENTERPRISE

PLAN PURPOSELY

PREPARE PRAYERFULLY

PROCEED POSITIVELY

PURSUE PERSISTENTLY

PERSEVERE PAINSTAKINGLY

PRESENT PERSUASIVELY

POTENTIALS & POSSIBILITIES

PROTECT AND PRESERVE

Steve Jobs says Stay foolish, Stay hungry

In the learning curve of risk – the more the demand, proportionally the more the supply. The cost of effort we give now in means of time and money, tears, sweat and blood has its corresponding ultimate rewards.

But in our business of input and output, the higher the risk is, the better the reward.

Which part of the balance you throw your weight.

It's up to you to roll on the dice of your life.

The Academia hybrid-brand of dealing with the challenges in life

My grandpa – Simplicity

Doc Tom Sr. – Academician   } **academia maxima**

Doc Tom Jr. – Financial juggernaut

Ladies and gentlemen we are all in the bandwagon of doing an innovative business together. You and I as one, doing our business together. We are not the faint-hearted entrepreneurs but the risk takers of **GO88**. Let us roll our sleeves and tonight is simply our affirmative commitment with food dance and entertainment. Altogether Alright and toast to a more and brighter tomorrow for all of us!

Thank you all!

REAL ESTATE APPRAISAL TERMS

Absorption Rate - The ratio of the number of properties in an area that have been sold against the number available in a particular market. Can be broken down to different types and sizes of properties. These rates are used to show the volatility of a market.

Abstraction Method - A Method of estimating the value of property using similar properties available in the same market to determine the value of a parcel of land. It is a structured analysis to systematically examine demand factors needed to support any increase in supply of real estate space in any given area.

Accessory Building - A structure on a property that serves a special purpose or complements the home or main building like a garage or shed is an accessory building. In most zoning districts an accessory building can be erected unattached from the house or main building.

Accretion - The natural growth of a piece of land resulting from forces of nature or the gradual addition to the shore or bank of a waterway by deposits of sand or silt. This natural process of land addition on a stream, lake or seaside is a special gift from mother nature to the land owner.

Acre - A tract of land containing 43,560 square feet, or 0.0016 square miles of land. An acre measures 208.71 feet on each side. In the metric system, one acre equals 0.4047 hectare or 40.47 area.

Actual Age - In appraisal terms the chronological age of an improvement, as contrasted with its Effective Age. Example: Although the actual age of the building was only 5 years, excessively heavy use made it appear much older. When purchasing insurance on your property, you will need to know the actual age.

Adjusted Sales Price - The adjusted sales price is an adjustment of the selling price of a property, sometimes used to match the characteristics of another property. Since no two parcels of land are exactly the same, an appraiser will analyze a other sales to find patterns, and assign dollar amounts to the main differences and then adjust the selling price. An example is two homes, next door to each other and looking exactly the same except one might have a garage attached. A momentary amount will be assigned to the garage. This amount will add to the selling price. The difference in the selling price would be the adjusted sales price

Aesthetic Value - Increment of market or user value attributed to the appearance of a property. Example: The lake and mountain setting of the vacation cabin contributed a great amount of aesthetic value to the property. A tennis court, swimming pool or beautiful landscaping can also increase the value of a property and allow the owner to obtain more of a premium price.

Amenity - Any feature of a property that increases its value or desirability. These might include natural amenities such as location or proximity to mountains, or man-made amenities like swimming pools, parks or other recreation. Might also include proximity to schools, libraries and shopping.

Amortization - To reduce a debt by regular payments of both principal and interest, as opposed to interest only payment. The operation of paying off indebtedness, such as a mortgage, by installments.

Annual Percentage Rate - The interest rate reflecting the cost of a mortgage as a yearly rate. This rate might be higher than the stated note rate or advertised rate on the mortgage, because it takes into account point and other credit cost. the APR allows home buyers to compare different types of mortgages based on the annual cost for each loan.

Annuity - An Annuity is a form of an investment that is typically provided by an insurance company. An annuity guarantees payments of pre-set amounts and pre-set times, money paid at regular intervals, often annuity.

Appraisal - A defensible and carefully documented opinion of value. Most commonly derived using recent sales of comparable properties by a licensed, professional appraiser. Not only used for real estate, but also used to appraise estates for tax purposes or inheritance.

Appraisal Foundation - A not-for-profit educational organization established by the appraisal profession in the United States in 1987. It is dedicated to the advancement of professional valuation and responsible for establishing, improving, and promoting the Uniform Standards of Professional Appraisal Practice (USPAP).

Appraisal Principles - The basic building blocks of the property valuation process, including property inspection, market analysis and basic economics.

Appraisal Report - The end result of the appraisal process and the purpose of the report is to convey the opinion of value of the subject property and support that opinion with corroborating information.

Appraisal Standards Board (ASB) - An independent board of the APPRAISAL FOUNDATION, which writes, amends, and interprets USPAP. The ASB is composed of up to seven appraisers appointed by the Foundation's Board of Trustees. The ASB holds public meetings throughout the year to interpret and amend USPAP.

Appraised Value - An opinion of the fair market value of a property as developed by a licensed, certified appraiser following accepted appraisal principals.

Appraiser - An educated, certified professional with extensive knowledge of real estate markets, values and practices. The appraiser is often the only independent voice in any real estate transaction with no vested interest in the ultimate value or sales price of the property.

Appreciation - The natural rise in property value due to market forces, or another way to describe appreciation is the increase in value of a property over time due to inflation,

Arms Length Transaction - Any transaction in which the two parties are unconnected and have no overt common interests. Such a transaction most often reflects the true market value of a property.

Assessed Value - The value of a property according to jurisdictional tax assessment.

Assessment - The function of assigning a value to a property for the purpose of levying taxes.

Assessment Ratio - The comparative relationship of a property's assessed value to its market value.

Assessor - The jurisdictional official who performs the assessment and assigns the value of a property.

Attached Housing - Any number of houses or other dwellings which are physically attached to one another, but are occupied by a number of different people. The individual houses may or may not be owned by separate people as well.

Backfill - Soil that is used to create a retaining wall on all or part of a property, or the slope of ground around a house, material placed adjacent to the retaining wall.

Blighted Area - Any region of a city or town that has fallen into disrepair or otherwise has become undesirable.

Bridge Financing - An interim loan made to facilitate the purchase of a new home before the buyer's current residence sells and its equity is available to fund the new purchase

Buffer Zone - A segment of land between two disparate municipal zones which acts as a shield to keep one zone from encroaching upon the other. Often used to separate residential districts from commercial areas.

Building Code - Regulations that ensure the safety and material compliance of new construction within a municipality. Building codes are localized to ensure they are adequate to meet the risk of common hazards.

Building Line Setback - The statutory distance between buildings and the property line, imposed by municipalities, home associations, or other agreements.

Bungalow - A one-story, home-style dating from the early twentieth century. Often characterized by a low-pitched roof.

Capital - Accumulated goods and money which is most often used to generate additional income. The assets of a business that can be applied to its operation. The amount of current assets that exceeds current liabilities

Capital Expenditure - An outlay of funds designed to improve the income-producing capabilities of an asset or to extend its economic life. Money spent to acquire or upgrade physical assets such as buildings and machinery.

Caveat Emptor - Literally translated: ''Let the buyer beware.'' A common business tenet whereby the buyer is responsible for verifying any and all claims by the seller of property.

Certified General Appraiser -Generally, any professional who has met the local or -state requirements, and passed the appropriate certification exam, and is capable of appraising any type of property.

Certified Residential Appraiser -A sub-classification of appraiser who is only licensed to appraise residential property, usually up to four units.

Chain of Title - The complete history of ownership of a piece of property, An analysis of -the transfers of title to a piece of property over the years and a history of all of the documents that transfer title to a parcel of real property.

Chattel - Any personal property which is not attached to or an integral part of a property. Personal property. Chattel is not commonly taken into consideration when appraising the value of real property

Clear Title - Ownership of property that us not encumbered by any counter claim or lien, title that is not burdened with defects, legal questions as to who owns the property, a marketable title.

Commission - A percentage of the sales price or a fixed fee negotiated by an agent to compensate for the effort expended to sell or purchase property.

Common Area Assessments - Fees which are charged to the tenets or owners of properties to cover the costs of maintaining areas shared with other tenets or owners.

Common Areas - Any areas, such as entryways, foyers, pools, recreational facilities or the like, which are shared by the tenants or owners of property nearby. Commonly found in condominium, PUD or office spaces.

Community Property - In many jurisdictions, any property which has been acquired by a married couple. The ownership of the property is considered equal unless stipulated otherwise by both parties.

Comparables - An abbreviated term used by appraisers to describe properties which are similar in size, condition, location and amenities to a subject property whose value is being determined. The Uniform Standards of Professional Appraisal Practice (USPAP) establish clear guidelines for determining a comparable property.

Compound Interest - Interest paid on the principal amount, as well as any accumulated interest.

Condemnation - The official process by which a property is deemed to be uninhabitable or unusable due to internal damage or other external conditions.

Condominium - A development where individual units are owned, but common areas and amenities are shared equally by all owners.

Condominium Conversion - Commonly, the conversion of a rental property such as an apartment complex into a condominium-style complex where each unit is owned rather than leased.

Contiguous - Very close or connected in space or time; "contiguous events"; connecting without a break; within a common bounds" immediate contact"; "the immediate vicinity"; "the immediate past,

Date of Appraisal - The specific point in time as of which an appraiser designates the value of a home. Often stipulated as the date of inspection.

Debt Equity Ratio - The ratio of the amount a mortgagor still owes on a property to the amount of equity they have in the home. Equity is calculated at the fair-market value of the home, less any outstanding mortgage.

Deed of Trust - A document which transfers title in a property to a trustee, whose obligations and powers are stipulated. Often used in mortgage transactions.

Default - The condition in which a borrower has failed to meet the obligations of a loan or mortgage.

Delinquency - The state in which a borrower has failed to meet payment obligations on time. Overdue in payment: a delinquent account.

Depreciation - The natural decline in property value due to market forces or depletion of resources.

Detached Single-Family Home - A single building improvement intended to serve as a home for one family.

Distressed Property - A mortgaged property which has been foreclosed on.

Dwelling - A house or other building which serves as a home.

Earnest Money Deposit - A cash deposit made to a home seller to secure an offer to buy the property. This amount is often forfeited if the buyer decides to withdraw his offer.

Easement - The right of a non-owner of property to exert control over a portion or all of the property. For example, power companies often own an easement over residential properties for access to their power lines.

Economic Depreciation - The decline in property value caused by external forces, such as neighborhood blight or adverse development.

Economic Life - The amount of time which any income-producing property is able to provide benefits to its owner.

Effective Age - The subjective, estimated age of a property based on its condition, rather than the actual time since it was built. Excessive wear and tear can cause a property's effective age to be greater than its actual age.

Eminent Domain - The legal process whereby a government can take ownership of a piece of property in order to convert it to public use. Often, the property owner is paid fair-market value for the property.

Encroachment - A building or other improvement on one property which invades another property or restricts is usage. Building, or part of a building, or obstruction that physically intrudes upon, overlaps, or trespasses upon the property of another.

Encumbrance - A claim against a property, such as a mortgage, lien as a claim or liability against real estate. This can include deed restrictions, easements encroachments or licenses.

Equity - The difference between the fair market value of a property and that amount an owner owes on any mortgages or loans secured by the property.

Equity Buildup - The natural increase in the amount of equity an owner has in a property, accumulated through market appreciation and debt repayment.

Escrow - An amount retained by a third party in a trust to meet a future obligation. Often used in the payment of annual taxes or insurance for real property.

Escrow Analysis - An analysis performed by the lender usually once each year to see that the amount of money going into the escrow account each month is correct for the forecasted expenses.

Estate - Total of all property and assets owned by an individual, Estate is a term used in the common law. It signifies the total of a person's property (including money), entitlements and obligations. It may also be used in reference to real estate at type of real property as an estate in land.

Examination of Title - A review which reveals the previous owners of, and the encumbrances on a piece of real estate. To conduct this review, a settlement agent must search the public records or examine an abstract

Exclusive Listing - An agreement between the owner of a property and a real estate agent giving the agent exclusive right to sell the property.

Façade - The front exposure of any building. Often used to describe an artificial or false front which is not consistent with the construction of the rest of the building

Fair Market Value - The price at which two unrelated parties, under no duress, are willing to transact business.

Fascia - A horizontal band or board, often used to conceal the ends of rafters; the front of an object. Part of the face of a building, where the shop or occupier's name is usually displayed., a flat, horizontal board enclosing the overhang under the eave.

Fee Appraiser - A certified, professional appraiser who forms an opinion of the fair market value of property and receives a set fee in exchange.

Fee Simple - A complete, unencumbered ownership right in a piece of property.

Fee Simple Estate - A form or ownership, or holding title to real estate. It is the most complete form of title, having an unconditional and unlimited interest of perpetual duration.

Final Value Estimate - The opinion of value of a piece of property resulting from an appraisal following the USPAP guidelines.

Fixture - Any piece of personal property which becomes permanently affixed to a piece of real property.

Floor Plan - The representation of a building which shows the basic outline of the structure, as well as detailed information about the positioning of rooms, hallways, doors, stairs and other features. Often includes detailed information about other fixtures and amenities.

Foreclosure - The process whereby a lender can claim the property used by a borrower to secure a mortgage and sell the property to meet the obligations of the loan. Legal process by which a mortgagor of property is deprived of his interest in that property due to failure to comply with payment terms and conditions of the mortgage, A court action.

Foundation - The solid structural element upon which a structure is built.

Frontage - The segment of a property that runs along a point of access, such as a street or water front.

Functional Obsolescence - A decrease in the value of property due to a feature or lack thereof which renders the property undesirable. Functional obsolescence can also occur when the surrounding area changes, rendering the property unusable for its originally intended purpose

General Lien - A broad-based claim against several properties owned by a defaulting party, with an attachment that gives the lender the right to seize the personal property of a borrower who has defaulted on the obligations of a loan, but prevents the lender from seizing real property.

Grade - The slope of land around a building. Also ground level.

Gross Area - The sum total of all floor space, including areas such as stairways and closet space. Often measured based on external wall lengths.

Height Zoning - A municipal restriction on the maximum height of any building or other structure.

Hidden Amenities - Assets of a property which contribute to its value, but are not readily apparent. Examples might include upgraded or premium building materials.

Highest and Best Use - The most profitable and likely use of a property. Selected from reasonably probable and legal alternative uses, which are found to be physically possible, appropriately supported and financially feasible to result in the highest possible land value.

Home Inspection - A complete examination of a building to determine its structural integrity and uncover any defects in materials or workmanship which may adversely affect the property or decrease its value.

Income Approach - The process of estimating the value of property by considering the present value of a stream of income generated by the property.

Income Property - A piece of property whose highest and best use is the generation of income through rents or other sources.

Independent Appraisal - An estimate of the value of a property prepared by someone who has no interest in the property or, if a mortgage is involved.

Inspection - The examination of a piece of property, its buildings or other amenities.

Interest Rate - A percentage of a loan or mortgage value that is paid to the lender as compensation for loaning funds.

Investment Property - Any piece of property that is expected to generate a financial return. This may come as the result of periodic rents or through appreciation of the property value over time.

Joint Tenancy - A situation where two or more parties own a piece of property together. Each of the owners has an equal share, and may not dispose of or alter that share without the consent of the other owners.

Judicial Foreclosure - A type of foreclosure conducted as a civil suit in a court of law.

Latent Defects - Any defect in a piece of property which is not readily apparent, but which has an impact of the value. Structural damage or termite infestation would be examples of latent defects.

Lease - A contract between a property owner and a tenant specifying the payment amount, terms and conditions, as well as the length of time the contract will be in force.

Leasehold Estate - A type of property "ownership" where the buyer actually has a long-term lease on the property.

Lease Option - A lease agreement that gives the tenant an option to buy the property. Usually, a portion of the regular monthly rent payment will be applied towards the down payment.

Legal Description - The description of a piece of property, identifying its specific location in terms established by the municipality or other jurisdiction in which the property resides. Often related in specific distances from a known landmark or intersection

Lien - Any claim against a piece of property resulting from a debt or other obligation.

Loan-to-Value Ratio (LTV) - The comparison of the amount owed on a mortgaged property to its fair market value.

Major Deficiency - A deficiency that strongly impacts the usability and habitability of a house. Or a deficiency that may be very expensive to repair.

Marginal Land - Land whose value has been diminished due to some internal defect or external condition. In most cases, the cost to correct the flaw or condition is as much or more than the expected return from the property.

Maturity - The date on which the principal balance of a financial instrument becomes due and payable.

Metes and Bounds - A traditional way of describing property, generally expressed in terms of distance from a known landmark or intersection, and then following the boundaries of the property back to its origin.

Mineral Rights - The legal right to exploit and enjoy the benefits of any minerals located below the surface of a parcel of land.

Natural Vacancy Rate - The percentage of vacant properties in a given area that is the result of natural turnover and market forces.

Neighborhood - A subsection of a municipality that has been designated by a developer, economic forces or physical formations.

Net Leasable Area - The space in a development, outside of the common areas, that can be rented to tenants.

Obsolescence - The process of an assets value diminishing due to the development of more desirable alternatives or because of the degradation of its capabilities.

Occupancy Rate - The percentage of properties in a given area that are occupied.

Open Space - Any land which has not had any significant buildings or structures erected on it. Most often used to describe desirable neighborhood features like parks or wooded areas.

Personal Property - Owned items which are not permanently affixed to the land.

Planned Unit Development (PUD) - A coordinated, real estate development where common areas are shared and maintained by an owner's association or other entity.

Plat - A plan or chart of a piece of land which lays out existing or planned streets, lots or other improvements.

Real Estate - A piece of land and any improvements or fixtures located on that land.

Real Property - Land, improvements and appurtenances, and the interest and benefits thereof.

Repayment Plan - A plan to repay delinquent payments, agreed upon between a lender and borrower, in an effort to avoid foreclosure.

Residential Property - A piece of property whose highest and best use is the maintenance of a residence.

Rights of First Refusal - An agreement giving a person the first opportunity to buy or lease a property before the owner offers it for sale to others.

Sale Price - The actual price a property sells for, exclusive of any special financing concessions.

Sales Comparison Approach - An appraisal practice which estimates the value of a property by comparing it to comparable properties which have sold recently within the sale area.

Scarcity - An economic principal that dictates the price of a good or service through the interaction of supply and demand. When an item is scarce, its price tends to rise, given a constant demand. Real Estate is a classic example of scarcity.

Subdivision - A residential development that is created from a piece of land which has been subdivided into individual lots.

Subject Property - A term which indicates a property which is being appraised.

Survey - A specific map of a piece of property which includes the legal boundaries and any improvements or features of the land. Surveys also depict any rights-of-way, encroachments or easements.

Tenancy in Common - A form of holding title, whereby there are two or more people on title to a property, ownership does not pass on to the others upon the death of one individual.

Under Improved Land - A piece of land which has been improved, but not to the full extent of its potential.

Unencumbered Property - Any property which has no outstanding claims or liens against it.

Useful Life - The span of time over which a property can be used or can provide benefits to its owner.

Vacancy Rate - The current percentage of vacant properties in a given area, regardless of why they are vacant.

Walk-Through Inspection - A process whereby an appraiser examines a property in preparation for estimating its value. Also, the process of inspecting a property for any damage prior to that property being bought or sold.

Wear and Tear - A term used to indicate the normal damage inflicted on a property through every-day use.

Zone - A specific area within a municipality or other jurisdiction which conforms to certain guidelines regarding the use of property in the zone. Typical zones include single-family, multi-family, industrial, commercial and mixed-use.

ECONOMICS-FINANCE TERMS

Accounting - Process of recording, measuring, interpreting, and communicating financial data for the purpose of decision making.

Accounts payable - Amounts due to others for goods and services purchased. They are usually payable within 12 months

Accounts receivable - Amounts due from others for goods and services delivered in the normal course of business.

Accounts receivable turnover - Measurement arrived at by dividing annual net sales by the average accounts receivable.

Accumulated depreciation - The cumulative charges against the fixed assets of a company for wear and tear or obsolescence.

Acid test ratio - Stringent test of liquidity; also called quick ratio. The ratio is found by dividing the most liquid current assets by current liabilities.

Acquisition cost - Price paid to buy goods, services, or assets. It equals the list price plus normal incidental costs to acquire the item, such as taxes, preparation, transportation, and installation.

Ad valorem tax - A tax based on the value or assessed value of property.

Amortization - Either the retirement of debt on an installment or serial payment basis, or the process of systematically charging off the cost of an intangible asset as goodwill, systems development, copyright over its estimated useful life.

Annuity - Series of equal periodic payments or receipts--for example, an investment that upon maturing provides payments of a fixed amount over a regular recurring period.

Asset - Anything of monetary value that is owned by a person.

Asset turnover - Ratio revealing the efficiency of an entity's assets in generating revenue.

Average total cost - The sum of all the production costs divided by the number of units produced.

Bear - An investor with a pessimistic market outlook; an investor who expects prices to fall and so sells now in order to buy later at a lower price.

Boom - A state of economic prosperity.

Break even - This is a term used to describe a point at which revenues equal costs (fixed and variable).

Balance sheet - Statement showing an entity's financial position at a certain date. It forms part of the financial statement.

Benchmark - A study to compare actual performance to a standard of typical competence; or, a standard for the basis of comparison as being above, below or comparable to.

Breakeven analysis – An analysis that determines the break-even sales or cash point, or the level of sales at which total costs equal total revenue. A break-even chart plots sales revenue, variable costs, and fixed costs on the vertical axis and volume on the horizontal axis. The break-even point is the point at which the total sales revenue line intersects the total cost line.

Breakeven point - The volume point at which revenues and costs are equal; a combination of sales and costs that will yield a no profit/no loss operation.

Capital asset - Asset purchased for use in production over a long period rather than for resale. Capital assets include land, buildings, plant and equipment, mineral deposits, and timber reserves.

Capitalization - The statement of capital within the firm - either in the form of money, common stock, long-term debt, or in some combination of all three.

Cash flow - Net amount of money generated or used from a given operation or asset for a given period.

Cash flow statement - Statement showing where a firm's cash comes from and on what it is spent. The net result is reflected in the balance of the cash account as of a certain date.

Capital - Wealth in the form of money or property owned by a person or business and human resources of economic value.

Capital gains tax - Tax paid on the gain realized upon the sale of an asset.

Comparative advantage - The ability to produce a good at a lower cost, relative to other goods, compared to another country. With perfect competition and undistorted markets, countries tend to export goods in which they have a Comparative Advantage and hence make gains from trading

Compound interest - Interest paid on the original principal and on interest accrued from time it became due.

Cost benefit analysis - A technique that assesses projects through a comparison between their costs and benefits, including social costs and benefits for an entire region or country. Depending on the project objectives and its the expected outputs, three types of CBA are generally recognised: financial; economic; and social. Generally cost-benefit analyses are comparative, i.e. they are used to compare alternative proposals. Cost-benefit analysis compares the costs and benefits of the situation with and without the project; the costs and benefits are considered over the life of the project.

Cost - The amount of money that must be paid to take ownership of something; expense or purchase price.

Cost-benefit analysis - The method of measuring the benefits anticipated from a decision by determining the cost of the decision, then deciding whether the benefit outweighs the cost of that decision.

Cost analysis - Examination of the cost of producing a particular product, normally undertaken before a project is begun.

Cost estimate - Forecast of probable cost to be incurred in the future.

Cost of capital - Calculated as a weighted average of the interest costs of debt and equity capital. Equity funds include both capital stock (common and preferred stock) and retained earnings.

Cost of sales - Generally, the cost of goods sold during a given accounting period.

Credit risk - The risk that a counter party to a financial transaction will fail to fulfill their obligation.

Creditor - The entities to which a debt is owed by another entity.

Current price - Prices prevailing during the current accounting period. They are nominal prices (i.e., unadjusted) and should not be confused with present prices.

Current ratio - A comparison of current assets to current liabilities, is a commonly used measure of short-run solvency, i.e., the immediate ability of a firm to pay its current debts as they come due.

Debt - The amount due by a customer in respect of goods supplied or services rendered by you.

Debt financing - Raising money through selling bonds, notes, or mortgages or borrowing directly from financial institutions.

Depreciation - The amount of expense charged against earnings by a company to write off the cost of a plant or machine over its useful live, giving consideration to wear and tear, obsolescence, and salvage value.

Deflation - A reduction in the level of national income and output, usually accompanied by a fall in the general price level.

Disclosure - An accounting principle that requires full (adequate) disclosure of all material (significant) matters affecting the financial statements that would be of interest to a concerned investor or creditor.

Discount rate - Interest rate used to convert future receipts or payments to their present value. The cost of capital may be used as the discount rate under the net present value method.

Dividend - Distribution of earnings paid to stockholders based on the number of shares they own. The most typical type is cash, but dividends may also be issued in such forms as stock and property.

Econometrics - The application of statistical and mathematical methods in the field of economics to test and quantify economic theories and the solutions to economic problems.

Economic development - The process of improving the quality of human life through increasing per capita income, reducing poverty, and enhancing individual economic opportunities. It is also sometimes defined to include better education, improved health and nutrition, conservation of natural resources, a cleaner environment, and a richer cultural life.

Economic growth - An increase in the nation's capacity to produce goods and services.

Economic infrastructure - The underlying amount of physical and financial capital embodied in roads, railways, waterways, airways, and other forms of transportation and communication plus water supplies, financial institutions, electricity, and public services such as health and education.

Economic integration - The merging to various degrees of the economies and economic policies of two or more countries in a given region. See also common market, customs union, free-trade area, trade creation, and trade diversion.

Elasticity of demand - The degree to which consumer demand for a product or service responds to a change in price, wage or other independent variable. When there is no perceptible response, demand is said to be inelastic.

Exchange rate - The price of one currency stated in terms of another currency.

Fixed costs - A cost incurred in the general operations of the business that is not directly attributable to the costs of producing goods and services. These "Fixed" or "Indirect" costs of doing business will be incurred whether or not any sales are made during the period, thus the designation "Fixed", as opposed to "Variable".

Economic internal rate of return (EIRR) - The rate of return that would be achieved on all project resource costs, where all benefits and costs are measured in economic prices.

Economic viability - The assessment that increases in output produced by a project using the least cost method will recover costs, provide an additional required rate of return, and sustain effective production in the face of uncertainty and risk.

Enterprise - An organization created for business ventures.

Entity - In business, is a separate or self-contained existence that provides goods or services.

Equity - The residual interest in the assets of the entity after deducting all its liabilities.

Gross domestic product - The total of goods and services produced by a nation over a given period, usually 1 year. Gross Domestic Product measures the total output from all the resources located in a country.

Gross national product - The value of all final goods and services produced within a nation in a given year, plus income earned by its citizens abroad, minus income earned by foreigners from domestic production.

Financial analysis - Transformation of financial data into a form that can be used to monitor and evaluate an entity's financial position, plan future financing, and assess the entity's size and growth rate.

Financial forecast - Financial projection that assumes a most probable or realistic scenario.

Financial Internal Rate of Return - The rate of return that would be achieved on all project costs, where all costs are measured in financial prices and when benefits represent the financial revenues that would accrue to the main project participant.

Financial model - Mathematical model describing the relationships among financial variables of a firm. A functional branch of a general corporate planning model, it is used essentially to generate pro forma financial statements and financial ratios.

Financial projection - Essential element of planning; the basis for budgeting and estimating future financing needs of a firm.

Financial ratio - Mathematical relationship between financial variables of business.

Financial statement - Statement containing financial information about an organization, usually includes a balance sheet, income statement, sources and applications of funds statement (sometimes referred to as a cash flow or funds flow statement) and the notes to the financial statements.

Fixed asset - Item that has physical substance and an economic life in excess of one year. It is bought for use in the operation of the business and not intended for resale to customers. With the exception of land, fixed assets are subject to depreciation.

Free cash flow - Net income plus non-cash charges to income, specifically depreciation and amortization less capital expenditures, to sustain the basic business.

Going concern - An enterprise that is normally viewed as continuing in operation for the foreseeable future, having neither the intention nor the necessity of liquidating or materially curtailing the scale of its operations.

Gross margin - The ratio of gross profit to sales revenue. (sometimes used as a synonym for gross profit). For a manufacturer, gross margin is a measure of a company's efficiency in turning raw materials into income; for a retailer it measures their markup over wholesale. Gross margin is gross income divided by net sales, expressed as a percentage.

Gross National Product (GNP) - The total dollar value of all final goods and services produced for consumption in society during a particular time period.

Gross sales - Total sales before sales discounts and sales returns and allowances. It equals total unit sales times the selling price per unit.

Growth rate - The percentage change per period (typically per year).

Hyper inflation - Situation in which a country experiences a cumulative inflation rate over three years approaching or exceeding 100 percent.

Imperfect competition - A market situation or structure in which producers have some degree of control over the price of their product. Examples include monopoly and oligopoly. See also perfect competition.

Imperfect market - A market where the theoretical assumptions of perfect competition are violated by the existence of, for example, a small number of buyers and sellers, barriers to entry, non homogeneity of products, and incomplete information. The three imperfect markets commonly analyzed in economic theory are monopoly, oligopoly, and monopolistic competition.

Index of industrial production: A quantity index that is designed to measure changes in the physical volume or production levels of industrial goods over time.

Inflation is the percentage increase in the prices of goods and services.

International poverty line - An arbitrary international real income measure, usually expressed in constant dollars (e.g., $270), used as a basis for estimating the proportion of the world's population that exists at bare levels of subsistence.

Income - (a) During an accounting period, revenue earned that results in an increase in total assets. (b) Revenue arising from sales of goods and services. (c) Excess of revenue over expenses and losses for an accounting period (i.e., net income).

Income statement - Form showing the elements used in arriving at an entity's net income for the accounting period; also called a profit and loss statement. Also called result of operations.

Inflation - An increase in the general price level of goods and services; alternatively, a decrease in the purchasing power of the dollar or other currency.

Inflation rate - The annual rate of change of the price index.

Intangible asset - Right or other nonphysical resource that is presumed to represent an advantage to a firm in the marketplace. Such assets include copyrights, patents, trademarks, goodwill, technical information, capitalized advertising costs, organization costs, licenses, leases, franchises, exploration permits, and import and export permits.

Interest - In law, is a right or legal share of something or a financial involvement with something; in finance, it is a fixed charge for borrowing money; usually a percentage of the amount borrowed.

Interest rate - The rate of interest charged for the use of money, usually expressed as an annual rate. The rate is derived by dividing the amount of interest by the amount of principal borrowed.

Internal Rate of Return (IRR) - Rate of return that equates the present value of future cash flows to the initial investment. Also referred to as the yield on investments.

Investment - The purchase of real property, stocks, bonds, collectible annuities, mutual fund shares, etc, with the expectation of realizing income or capital gain, or both, in the future. Investment is longer term and usually less risky than speculation.

Joint venture - Specific business undertaken jointly by two or more entities. Joint ventures are often formed when one party lacks technological expertise, financial resources, government ties, a distribution network, or manufacturing capability.

Lease - A contract where a party being the owner (lessor) of an asset (leased asset) provides the asset for use by the lessee at a consideration (rentals), either fixed or dependent on any variables, for a certain period

Leverage - Ability of fixed costs to magnify returns to a firm's owners. operating leverage, a measure of operating risk, refers to the fixed operating costs found in a firm's income statement. financial leverage, a measure of financial risk, refers to financing

Liability - Present obligation of the entity arising from past events, the settlement of which is expected to result in and outflow from the entity of the resources embodying economic benefits.

Liquid asset - Cash and any asset that can quickly be converted into cash (e.g., cash, checks and easily convertible securities).

Liquidation - Process of closing a business entity, including selling or disposing of the assets, paying the liabilities, and returning the balance (if any) to the owners.

Liquidity ratio - Measures of a business entity's liquidity, such as the current ratio, acid test ratio, accounts receivable turnover, and inventory turnover .

Loan - An agreement under which an owner of assets (the lender) allows another entity (the borrower) to use the assets for a specified time period.

Long-term asset - Asset whose future benefit is expected for a number of years; includes such non-current assets as buildings and equipment.

Macroeconomics: The branch of economics that considers the relationships among broad economic aggregates such as national income, total volumes of saving, investment, consumption expenditure, employment, and money supply. It is also concerned with determinants of the magnitudes of these aggregates and their rates of change over time.

Market economy - A free private-enterprise economy governed by consumer sovereignty, a price system, and the forces of supply and demand.

Market prices - Prices established by demand and supply in a free-market economy.

Microeconomics - The branch of economics concerned with individual decision units-- firms and households--and the way in which their decisions interact to determine relative prices of goods and factors of production and how much of these will be bought and sold.

Monopoly - A market situation in which a product that does not have close substitutes is being produced and sold by a single seller.

Market price - Price at which a security or commodity is quoted or offered for sale.

Market risk - The risk that the value of your investment will decrease due to moves in market factors.

Market value - In general, is the price at which buyers and sellers trade similar items in an open marketplace.

Maturity risk - Maturity risk relates to mismatching of investments and borrowing operations.

Money market - Market for short-term debt instruments, such as certificates of deposit, commercial paper, banker's acceptances, U.S. Treasury bills, and discount notes.

Newly industrializing countries (NICs) A small group of countries at a relatively advanced level of economic development with a substantial and dynamic industrial sector and with close links to the international trade, finance, and investment system (Argentina, Brazil, Greece, Mexico, Portugal, Singapore, South Korea, Spain, and Taiwan).

Nongovernmental organizations (NGOs) - Privately owned and operated organizations involved in providing financial and technical assistance to LDCs. See foreign aid.

Net assets - The difference between total assets and current liabilities including non capitalized long term liabilities.

Net cash flow - Equals cash receipts minus cash payments over a given period of time; or equivalently, net profit plus amounts charged off for depreciation, depletion, and amortization.

Net income - Gross income from all sources less all administrative and operating expenditures, depreciation, taxes, and interest and other charges on debt.

Net operating income - Income after deducting for operating expenses but before deducting for income taxes and interest.

Net present value (NPV) - A method used in evaluating investments, whereby the net present value of all cash outflows (such as the cost of the investment) and cash inflows (returns) is calculated using a given discount rate, usually required rate of return. An investment is acceptable if the NPV is positive.

Net worth - Total assets less total liabilities. Net worth represents shareholder equity.

Nominal interest rate - Contracted or stated interest rate, not deflated for price-level changes.

Official development assistance (ODA) Net disbursements of loans or grants made on concessional terms by official agencies of member countries of the Organization for Economic Cooperation and Development (OECD).

Organization for Economic Cooperation and Development (OECD) - An organization of 20 countries from the Western world including all of those in Europe and North America. Its major objective is to assist the economic growth of its member nations by promoting cooperation and technical analysis of national and international economic trends.

Objective - A statement that is written in terms of specific measurable time-based and verifiable outcomes that challenge the organization to be more responsive to the environment to achieve the desired goals.

Obsolescence - Reduction or cessation of an asset's usefulness, resulting from technological or market changes, wear and tear from use, or natural deterioration. Obsolescence is a major factor in determining depreciation.

Operating cost - Expenses incurred in the day-to-day running of a company.

Operating expenses - All selling and general & administrative expenses. Includes depreciation, but not interest expense.

Operating income - Revenue less cost of goods sold and related operating expenses that are applied to the day-to-day operating activities of the company. It excludes financial related items (i.e., interest income, dividend income, and interest expense), extraordinary items, and taxes.

Operating ratio - Measures a firm's operating efficiency; calculated: company operating expenses divided by its operating revenues.

Opportunity cost - The benefit foregone from not using a good or resource in its best alternative use.

Overhead cost - Cost of materials or services not directly traceable to a specific product but necessary for the productive or administrative process. Examples of such costs include general office salaries and apportioned costs of premises shared by multiple activities.

Owners' equity - Interest of the owners in the assets of the business; the interest is represented by capital contributions and retained earnings.

Perfect competition - A market situation characterized by the existence of very many buyers and sellers of homogeneous goods or services with perfect knowledge and free entry so that no single buyer or seller can influence the price of the good or service.

Poverty line - A level of income below, which people are deemed poor. A global poverty line of $1 per person per day was suggested in 1990 (World Bank 1990). This line facilitates comparison of how many poor people there are in different countries.

Price - The monetary or real value of a resource, commodity, or service. The role of prices in a market economy is to ration or allocate resources in accordance with supply and demand; relative prices should reflect the relative scarcity of different resources, goods, or services.

Price elasticity of demand - The responsiveness of the quantity of a commodity demanded to a change in its price, expressed as the percentage change in quantity demanded divided by the percentage change in price.

Price elasticity of supply - The responsiveness of the quantity of a commodity supplied to a change in its price, expressed as the percentage change in quantity supplied divided by the percentage change in price.

Payback period - In capital budgeting, is the length of time needed to recoup the cost of capital investment. The payback period is the ratio of the initial investment (cash outlay, regardless of the source of the cash) to the annual cash inflows for the recovery period. The major shortcoming for the payback period method is that it does not take into account cash flows after the payback period and is therefore not a measure of the profitability of an investment project.

Present value - Discounted current worth of future cash flows from an investment. The discounted value of a payment or stream of payments to be received in the future, taking into consideration a specific interest or discount rate. Present Value represents a series of future cash flows expressed in today's dollars.

Profit margin - Ratio of net income to net sales.

Profitability - Company's ability to generate revenues in excess of the costs incurred in producing those revenues.

Profitability ratio - Measures of performance showing how much the firm is earning compared to its sales, assets or equity.

Project appraisal - The assessment of the viability of proposed long-term investments in terms of shareholder wealth.

Project cost table - A summary of base costs, physical contingencies, and price contingencies (and where appropriate, risk contingencies) to determine the estimated total cost of a Bank-financed project.

Projection - An approximation of future events. Usually a projection is made by extrapolating known information into the future period, considering events that could affect the outcome.

Quick ratio - (or Acid Test Ratio) a more rigorous test than the Current Ratio of short-run solvency, the current ability of a firm to pay its current debts as they come due.

Rate - Amount of money charged or paid, calculated according to a certain rule or ratio.

Rate of return - The gain or loss for a security in a particular period, consisting of income plus capital gains relative to investment, usually quoted as a percentage. The real rate of return is the annual return realized on that investment, adjusted for changes in the price due to inflation.

Ratio - Expression used to define a relationship between two or more factors; for example a current ratio that is used to report the relationship of operating income to operating expenditures

Real interest rate - Interest rate adjusted for inflation.

Retained earnings - Profits of the business that have not been paid out to the owners as of the balance sheet date. The earnings have been "retained" for use in the business (Retained Earnings is an account in the equity section of the balance sheet). It is comprised of the balance, either debit or credit, of appropriated or not appropriated earnings of an entity that are retained in the business.

Return on Assets - Shows the after tax earnings of assets. Return on assets is an indicator of how profitable a company is. Use this ratio annually to compare a business' performance to the industry norms: The higher the ratio the greater the return on assets. However this has to be balanced against such factors as risk, sustainability and reinvestment in the business through development costs.

Return on Equity - Measures the overall efficiency of the firm in managing its total investments in assets and in generating a return to stockholders. It is the primary measure of how well management is running the company.

Return on Investment (ROI) - A profitability measure that evaluates the performance of a business. ROI can be calculated in various ways. The most common method is Net Income as a percentage of Net Book Value (total assets minus intangible assets and liabilities).

Risk - The measurable possibility of losing or not gaining value. Risk is different from uncertainty. Uncertainty is not measurable.

Risk analysis - The analysis of project risks associated with the value of key project variables, and therefore the risk associated with the overall project result. Quantitative risk analysis considers the range of possible values for key variables, and the probability with which they may occur. Simultaneous and random variation within these ranges leads to a combined probability that the project will be unacceptable.

Risk management - The selection of those risks a business should take, and those which should be avoided or mitigated, followed by action to avoid or reduce risk.

Salvage value - a) Realizable value of a fixed asset after deducting costs associated with its sale; b) Scrap value or the value to a junk dealer; or c) The amount remaining after all depreciation has been deducted from the original cost of a depreciable asset.

Sensitivity analysis - The analysis of how sensitive outcomes are to changes in the assumptions. The assumptions that deserve the most attention should depend largely on the dominant benefit and cost elements and the areas of greatest uncertainty of the program or process being analyzed.

Sinking fund - Required annual payment to an asset account that is set apart for the amortization of debt, redemption of preferred stock, protection of an investment in depreciable property, or other specified purposes. A sinking fund may be held in cash or marketable securities until needed.

Solvency - Condition of a company able to satisfy its debt obligations as they fall due. Various financial ratios measure a company's degree of solvency, such as the debt-equity ratio and the debt service ratio.

Sovereign risk - Risk that a government will default on a loan or fail to honor other business commitments because of a change in national policy.

Straight-line depreciation - Allows an equal amount to be charged as depreciation for each year of the expected use of the asset. It is computed by dividing the adjusted basis of a property by the estimated number of years of remaining useful life.

Sustainability - Sustainability is the ability of a development activity to deliver substantial benefits for an extended period of time after financial, managerial and technical assistance from a donor finishes.

Takeover - Form of acquisition by one company of another; usually followed by a Merger. Takeover can be hostile or friendly. The public tender offer is a means of acquiring a target firm against the wishes of its management. In a friendly takeover, the acquiring firm negotiates with the targeted company and the subsequent agreement, reached in an amiable atmosphere, is put up for approval by shareholders.

Tangible asset - Normally refers to assets that can be held or seen and that are capable of being appraised at an actual or approximate value (e.g. inventory, land & buildings, etc.).

Tax - Compulsory levy imposed by the state/country to individual property or transaction use to defray necessary expenses of the government.

Turnover - Frequency with which an item (i.e., fixed asset, inventory, accounts receivable, personnel) is replaced during an accounting period.

VAT - A form of indirect sales tax paid on products and services at each stage of production or distribution, based on the value added at that stage and included in the cost to the ultimate customer.

Valuation - Approach by which the realistic value of an asset is determined for proper financial reporting. For example, accounts receivable from a credit sale transaction may be legitimate, but if the customer is bankrupt and unable to pay, the valuation is lower.

Value added - The difference, at each stage of production or the provisioning of a service, between the price of a product or service and all materials or activities paid for to produce the product or provide the service.

Variable costs - Expenses that vary in total in direct proportion to changes in activities, such as machine hours or labor hours within the relevant range. Examples are direct materials used to manufacture an item and gasoline expense based on mileage driven. Variable cost per unit is constant.

Viability - In economics, is the capability of developing and surviving as a relatively independent social, economic or political unit.

Value Added Tax (VAT) - A consumption tax where taxes are levied at each step of a manufacturing process where value is added to that product at that point in the manufacturing cycle; as well as at the point where the consumer purchases the end product.

Weighted Average Cost of Capital (WACC) - An average representing the expected return on all of a company's securities. Each source of capital, such as stocks, bonds, and other debt, is weighted in the calculation according to its prominence in the company's capital structure.

Working capital - Current assets minus current liabilities; also called net current assets or current capital. It measures the margin of protection for current creditors. It reflects the ability to finance current operations.

Working capital ratio - Working capital expressed as a percentage of sales.

Working ratio - Ratio of gross operating revenues from all operational sources to total operating expenditures, excluding depreciation and non-cash charges.

Yield - (a) On a security, the real rate of return to the investor or the effective cost to the issuer for a specified period. It differs from the coupon rate, since it takes into account the market price of the security. (b) Return from an asset or service provided.

Yield curve - Graph showing the term structure of interest rates by plotting the yields of all bonds of the same quality with maturities ranging from the shortest to the longest available. The resulting curve shows whether short-term rates are higher or lower than long-term rates.

Yield to maturity – Effective rate of return an investor will receive if a long-term, interest-bearing investment, such as a bond, is held to its maturity date.

BUSINESS VALUATION TERMS

The business valuation professional duty is to communicate the valuation process and conclusion, must be clear and not misleading. And do not depart from meanings that are clearly established and consistently applied throughout the profession.

If, in the opinion of the business valuation professional, one or more of these terms needs to be used in a manner that materially departs from the enclosed definitions, it is recommended that the term be defined as used within that valuation engagement.

The use of this glossary has been developed to guide guidance to business valuation practitioners.

Departure from which this glossary is not intended to provide a basis for civil liability and should not be presumed to create evidence that any duty has been breached.

Adjusted Book Value Method—a method within the asset approach whereby all assets and liabilities (including off-balance sheet, intangible, and contingent) are adjusted to their fair market values

Asset (Asset-Based) Approach—a general way of determining a value indication of a business, business ownership interest, or security using one or more methods based on the value of the assets net of liabilities.

Business Enterprise—a commercial, industrial, service, or investment entity (or a combination thereof) pursuing an economic activity.

Business Risk—the degree of uncertainty of realizing expected future returns of the business resulting from factors other than financial leverage.

Business Valuation—the act or process of determining the value of a business enterprise or ownership interest therein.

Capital Asset Pricing Model (CAPM)—a model in which the cost of capital for any stock or portfolio of stocks equals a risk-free rate plus a risk premium that is proportionate to the systematic risk of the stock or portfolio.

Capitalization—a conversion of a single period of economic benefits into value.

Capitalization Factor—any multiple or divisor used to convert anticipated economic benefits of a single period into value.

Capitalization of Earnings Method—a method within the income approach whereby economic benefits for a representative single period are converted to value through division by a capitalization rate.

Capitalization Rate—any divisor (usually expressed as a percentage) used to convert anticipated economic benefits of a single period into value.

Capital Structure—the composition of the invested capital of a business enterprise, the mix of debt and equity financing.

Cash Flow—cash that is generated over a period of time by an asset, group of assets, or business enterprise. It may be used in a general sense to encompass various levels of specifically defined cash flows. When the term is used, it should be supplemented by a qualifier (for example, "discretionary" or "operating") and a specific definition in the given valuation context.

Common Size Statements—financial statements in which each line is expressed as a percentage of the total. On the balance sheet, each line item is shown as a percentage of total assets, and on the income statement, each item is expressed as a percentage of sales.

Control—the power to direct the management and policies of a business enterprise.

Control Premium—an amount or a percentage by which the pro rata value of a controlling interest exceeds the pro rata value of a non-controlling interest in a business enterprise, to reflect the power of control.

Cost Approach—a general way of determining a value indication of an individual asset by quantifying the amount of money required to replace the future service capability of that asset.

Cost of Capital—the expected rate of return that the market requires in order to attract funds to a particular investment.

Discount for Lack of Control—an amount or percentage deducted from the pro rata share of value of 100% of an equity interest in a business to reflect the absence of some or all of the powers of control.

Discount for Lack of Marketability—an amount or percentage deducted from the value of an ownership interest to reflect the relative absence of marketability.

Discount for Lack of Voting Rights—an amount or percentage deducted from the per share value of a minority interest voting share to reflect the absence of voting rights.

Discount Rate—a rate of return used to convert a future monetary sum into present value.

Discounted Cash Flow Method—a method within the income approach whereby the present value of future expected net cash flows is calculated using a discount rate.

Discounted Future Earnings Method—a method within the income approach whereby the present value of future expected economic benefits is calculated using a discount rate.

Economic Benefits—inflows such as revenues, net income, net cash flows, etc.

Economic Life—the period of time over which property may generate economic benefits.

Equity—the owner's interest in property after deduction of all liabilities.

Equity Net Cash Flows—those cash flows available to pay out to equity holders (in the form of dividends) after funding operations of the business enterprise, making necessary capital investments, and increasing or decreasing debt financing.

Equity Risk Premium—a rate of return added to a risk-free rate to reflect the additional risk of equity instruments over risk free instruments (a component of the cost of equity capital or equity discount rate).

Excess Earnings—that amount of anticipated economic benefits that exceeds an appropriate rate of return on the value of a selected asset base (often net tangible assets) used to generate those anticipated economic benefits.

Excess Earnings Method—a specific way of determining a value indication of a business, business ownership interest, or security determined as the sum of a) the value of the assets derived by capitalizing excess earnings and b) the value of the selected asset base. Also frequently used to value intangible assets. See Excess Earnings.

Fair Market Value—the price, expressed in terms of cash equivalents, at which property would change hands between a hypothetical willing and able buyer and a hypothetical willing and able seller, acting at arms length in an open and unrestricted market, when neither is under compulsion to buy or sell and when both have reasonable knowledge of the relevant facts. {NOTE: In Canada, the term "price" should be replaced with the term "highest price"}

Fairness Opinion—an opinion as to whether or not the consideration in a transaction is fair from a financial point of view.

Financial Risk—the degree of uncertainty of realizing expected future returns of the business resulting from financial leverage. See Business Risk

Forced Liquidation Value—liquidation value, at which the asset or assets are sold as quickly as possible, such as at an auction.

Going Concern—an ongoing operating business enterprise.

Going Concern Value—the value of a business enterprise that is expected to continue to operate into the future. The intangible elements of Going Concern Value result from factors such as having a trained work force, an operational plant, and the necessary licenses, systems, and procedures in place.

Goodwill—that intangible asset arising as a result of name, reputation, customer loyalty, location, products, and similar factors not separately identified.

Goodwill Value—the value attributable to goodwill.

Guideline Public Company Method—a method within the market approach whereby market multiples are derived from market prices of stocks of companies that are engaged in the same or similar lines of business, and that are actively traded on a free and open market.

Income (Income-Based) Approach—a general way of determining a value indication of a business, business ownership interest, security, or intangible asset using one or more methods that convert anticipated economic benefits into a present single amount.

Intangible Assets—non-physical assets such as franchises, trademarks, patents, copyrights, goodwill, equities, mineral rights, securities and contracts (as distinguished from physical assets) that grant rights and privileges, and have value for the owner.

Internal Rate of Return—a discount rate at which the present value of the future cash flows of the investment equals the cost of the investment.

Intrinsic Value—the value that an investor considers, on the basis of an evaluation or available facts, to be the "true" or "real" value that will become the market value when other investors reach the same conclusion. When the term applies to options, it is the difference between the exercise price or strike price of an option and the market value of the underlying security.

Invested Capital—the sum of equity and debt in a business enterprise. Debt is typically a) all interest bearing debt or b) long-term interest-bearing debt. When the term is used, it should be supplemented by a specific definition in the given valuation context.

Invested Capital Net Cash Flows—those cash flows available to pay out to equity holders (in the form of dividends) and debt investors (in the form of principal and interest) after funding operations of the business enterprise and making necessary capital investments.

Investment Risk—the degree of uncertainty as to the realization of expected returns.

Investment Value—the value to a particular investor based on individual investment requirements and expectations. {NOTE: in Canada, the term used is "Value to the Owner"}.

Key Person Discount — an amount or percentage deducted from the value of an ownership interest to reflect the reduction in value resulting from the actual or potential loss of a key person in a business enterprise.

Limited Appraisal—the act or process of determining the value of a business, business ownership interest, security, or intangible asset with limitations in analyses, procedures, or scope.

Liquidity—the ability to quickly convert property to cash or pay a liability.

Liquidation Value—the net amount that would be realized if the business is terminated and the assets are sold piecemeal. Liquidation can be either "orderly" or "forced."

Majority Control—the degree of control provided by a majority position.

Majority Interest—an ownership interest greater than 50% of the voting interest in a business enterprise.

Market (Market-Based) Approach—a general way of determining a value indication of a business, business ownership interest, security, or intangible asset by using one or more methods that compare the subject to similar businesses, business ownership interests, securities, or intangible assets that have been sold.

Market Capitalization of Equity—the share price of a publicly traded stock multiplied by the number of shares outstanding.

Market Capitalization of Invested Capital—the market capitalization of equity plus the market value of the debt component of invested capital.

Market Multiple—the market value of a company's stock or invested capital divided by a company measure (such as economic benefits, number of customers).

Marketability—the ability to quickly convert property to cash at minimal cost.

Merger and Acquisition Method—a method within the market approach whereby pricing multiples are derived from transactions of significant interests in companies engaged in the same or similar lines of business.

Mid-Year Discounting—a convention used in the Discounted Future Earnings Method that reflects economic benefits being generated at midyear, approximating the effect of economic benefits being generated evenly throughout the year.

Minority Discount—a discount for lack of control applicable to a minority interest.

Minority Interest—an ownership interest less than 50% of the voting interest in a business enterprise.

Net Book Value—with respect to a business enterprise, the difference between total assets (net of accumulated depreciation, depletion, and amortization) and total liabilities as they appear on the balance sheet (synonymous with Shareholder's Equity). With respect to a specific asset, the capitalized cost less accumulated amortization or depreciation as it appears on the books of account of the business enterprise.

Net Cash Flows—when the term is used, it should be supplemented by a qualifier. See Equity Net Cash Flows and Invested Capital Net Cash Flows

Net Present Value—the value, as of a specified date, of future cash inflows less all cash outflows (including the cost of investment) calculated using an appropriate discount rate.

Net Tangible Asset Value—the value of the business enterprise's tangible assets (excluding excess assets and non-operating assets) minus the value of its liabilities.

Non-Operating Assets—assets not necessary to ongoing operations of the business enterprise. {NOTE: in Canada, the term used is "Redundant Assets"}.

Normalized Earnings—economic benefits adjusted for nonrecurring, noneconomic, or other unusual items to eliminate anomalies and/or facilitate comparisons.

Normalized Financial Statements—financial statements adjusted for non operating assets and liabilities and/or for nonrecurring, noneconomic, or other unusual items to eliminate anomalies and/or facilitate comparisons.

Orderly Liquidation Value – liquidation value at which the asset or assets are sold over a reasonable period of time to maximize proceeds received.

Premise of Value—an assumption regarding the most likely set of transactional circumstances that may be applicable to the subject valuation; e.g. going concern, liquidation.

Present Value—the value, as of a specified date, of future economic benefits and/or proceeds from sale, calculated using an appropriate discount rate.

Portfolio Discount—an amount or percentage deducted from the value of a business enterprise to reflect the fact that it owns dissimilar operations or assets that do not fit well together.

Price/Earnings Multiple—the price of a share of stock divided by its earnings per share.

Rate of Return—an amount of income (loss) and/or change in value realized or anticipated on an investment, expressed as a percentage of that investment.

Report Date—the date conclusions are transmitted to the client.

Replacement Cost New—the current cost of a similar new property having the nearest equivalent utility to the property being valued.

Reproduction Cost New—the current cost of an identical new property.

Required Rate of Return—the minimum rate of return acceptable by investors before they will commit money to an investment at a given level of risk.

Residual Value—the value as of the end of the discrete projection period in a discounted future earnings model.

Return on Equity—the amount, expressed as a percentage, earned on a company's common equity for a given period.

Return on Invested Capital—the amount, expressed as a percentage, earned on a company's total capital for a given period.

Risk-Free Rate—the rate of return available in the market on an investment free of default risk.

Risk Premium—a rate of return added to a risk-free rate to reflect risk.

Rule of Thumb—a mathematical formula developed from the relationship between price and certain variables based on experience, observation, hearsay, or a combination of these; usually industry specific.

Special Interest Purchasers – acquirers who believe they can enjoy post-acquisition economies of scale, synergies, or strategic advantages by combining the acquired business interest with their own.

Standard of Value – the identification of the type of value being utilized in a specific engagement; e.g. fair market value, fair value, investment value.

Sustaining Capital Reinvestment – the periodic capital outlay required to maintain operations at existing levels, net of the tax shield available from such outlays.

Systematic Risk – the risk that is common to all risky securities and cannot be eliminated through diversification. The measure of systematic risk in stocks is the beta coefficient.

Tangible Assets—physical assets (such as cash, accounts receivable, inventory, property, plant and equipment, etc.).

Unsystematic Risk – the portion of total risk specific to an individual security that can be avoided through diversification.

Valuation – the act or process of determining the value of a business, business ownership interest, security, or intangible asset.

Valuation Approach – a general way of determining a value indication of a business, business ownership interest, security, or intangible asset using one or more valuation methods.

Valuation Date – the specific point in time as of which the valuator's conclusion of value applies (also referred to as "Effective Date" or "Appraisal Date").

Valuation Method — within approaches, a specific way to determine value.

Valuation Procedure — the act, manner, and technique of performing the steps of an appraisal method.

Valuation Ratio – a fraction in which a value or price serves as the numerator and financial, operating, or physical data serve as the denominator.

Weighted Average Cost of Capital (WACC) – the cost of capital (discount rate) determined by the weighted average, at market value, of the cost of all financing sources in the business enterprise's capital structure.

International Glossary of Business Valuation Terms - NACVA - *www.nacva.com/content.asp*

GLOSSARY OF CLIMATE CHANGE TERMS

Abrupt Climate Change - Sudden (on the order of decades), large changes in some major component of the climate system, with rapid, widespread effects.

Adaptation - Adjustment or preparation of natural or human systems to a new or changing environment which moderates harm or exploits beneficial opportunities.

Adaptive Capacity - The ability of a system to adjust to climate change (including climate variability and extremes) to moderate potential damages, to take advantage of opportunities, or to cope with the consequences.

Afforestation - Planting of new forests on lands that historically have not contained forests.

Alternative Energy - Energy derived from nontraditional sources (e.g., compressed natural gas, solar, hydroelectric, wind).

Atmosphere - The gaseous envelope surrounding the Earth. The dry atmosphere consists almost entirely of nitrogen (78.1% volume mixing ratio) and oxygen (20.9% volume mixing ratio), together with a number of trace gases, such as argon (0.93% volume mixing ratio), helium, radiatively active greenhouse gases such as carbon dioxide (0.035% volume mixing ratio), and ozone. In addition the atmosphere contains water vapor, whose amount is highly variable but typically 1% volume mixing ratio.

Biofuels - Gas or liquid fuel made from plant material (biomass) Includes wood, wood waste, wood liquors, peat, railroad ties, wood sludge, spent sulfite liquors, agricultural waste, straw, tires, fish oils, tall oil, sludge waste, waste alcohol, municipal solid waste, landfill gases, other waste, and ethanol blended into motor gasoline.

Biomass - Materials that are biological in origin, including organic material (both living and dead) from above and below ground, for example, trees, crops, grasses, tree litter, roots, and animals and animal waste.

Biosphere - The part of the Earth system comprising all ecosystems and living organisms, in the atmosphere, on land (terrestrial biosphere) or in the oceans (marine biosphere), including derived dead organic matter, such as litter, soil organic matter and oceanic detritus.

Carbon Dioxide - A naturally occurring gas, and also a by-product of burning fossil fuels and biomass, as well as land-use changes and other industrial processes. It is the principal human caused greenhouse gas that affects the Earth's radiative balance. It is the reference gas against which other greenhouse gases are measured and therefore has a Global Warming Potential of 1.

Carbon Footprint - The total amount of greenhouse gases that are emitted into the atmosphere each year by a person, family, building, organization, or company. A persons carbon footprint includes greenhouse gas emissions from fuel that an individual burns directly, such as by heating a home or riding in a car. It also includes greenhouse gases that come from producing the goods or services that the individual uses, including emissions from power plants that make electricity, factories that make products, and landfills where trash gets sent.

Carbon Sequestration - Terrestrial, or biologic, carbon sequestration is the process by which trees and plants absorb carbon dioxide, release the oxygen, and store the carbon. Geologic sequestration is one step in the process of carbon capture and sequestration (CCS), and involves injecting carbon dioxide deep underground where it stays permanently.

Climate - Climate in a narrow sense is usually defined as the "average weather," or more rigorously, as the statistical description in terms of the mean and variability of relevant quantities over a period of time ranging from months to thousands of years. The classical period is 3 decades, as defined by the World Meteorological Organization (WMO). These quantities are most often surface variables such as temperature, precipitation, and wind. Climate in a wider sense is the state, including a statistical description, of the climate system.

Climate Change - Climate change refers to any significant change in the measures of climate lasting for an extended period of time. In other words, climate change includes major changes in temperature, precipitation, or wind patterns, among others, that occur over several decades or longer.

Concentration - Amount of a chemical in a particular volume or weight of air, water, soil, or other medium.

Deforestation - Those practices or processes that result in the conversion of forested lands for non-forest uses. Deforestation contributes to increasing carbon dioxide concentrations for two reasons: 1) the burning or decomposition of the wood releases carbon dioxide; and 2) trees that once removed carbon dioxide from the atmosphere in the process of photosynthesis are no longer present.

Desertification - Land degradation in arid, semi-arid, and dry sub-humid areas resulting from various factors, including climatic variations and human activities. Further, the UNCCD (The United Nations Convention to Combat Desertification) defines land degradation as a reduction or loss, in arid, semi-arid, and dry sub-humid areas, of the biological or economic productivity and complexity of rain-fed cropland, irrigated cropland, or range, pasture, forest, and woodlands resulting from land uses or from a process or combination of processes, including processes arising from human activities and habitation patterns, such as: (i) soil erosion caused by wind and/or water; (ii) deterioration of the physical, chemical and biological or economic properties of soil; and (iii) long-term loss of natural vegetation. Conversion of forest to non-forest.

Dryland Farming - A technique that uses soil moisture conservation and seed selection to optimize production under dry conditions.

Ecosystem - Any natural unit or entity including living and non-living parts that interact to produce a stable system through cyclic exchange of materials.

Emissions - The release of a substance (usually a gas when referring to the subject of climate change) into the atmosphere.

Emissions Factor - A unique value for scaling emissions to activity data in terms of a standard rate of emissions per unit of activity (e.g., grams of carbon dioxide emitted per barrel of fossil fuel consumed, or per pound of product produced).

Evaporation - The process by which water changes from a liquid to a gas or vapor.

Fossil Fuel - A general term for organic materials formed from decayed plants and animals that have been converted to crude oil, coal, natural gas, or heavy oils by exposure to heat and pressure in the earth's crust over hundreds of millions of years.

Geosphere - The soils, sediments, and rock layers of the Earth's crust, both continental and beneath the ocean floors.

Glacier - A multi-year surplus accumulation of snowfall in excess of snowmelt on land and resulting in a mass of ice at least 0.1 km2 in area that shows some evidence of movement in response to gravity. A glacier may terminate on land or in water. Glacier ice is the largest reservoir of fresh water on Earth, and second only to the oceans as the largest reservoir of total water. Glaciers are found on every continent except Australia.

Global Average Temperature - An estimate of Earths mean surface air temperature averaged over the entire planet.

Global Warming - The recent and ongoing global average increase in temperature near the Earths surface.

Global Warming Potential - A measure of the total energy that a gas absorbs over a particular period of time (usually 100 years), compared to carbon dioxide.

Greenhouse Effect - Trapping and build-up of heat in the atmosphere (troposphere) near the Earth's surface. Some of the heat flowing back toward space from the Earth's surface is absorbed by water vapor, carbon dioxide, ozone, and several other gases in the atmosphere and then reradiated back toward the Earth's surface. If the atmospheric concentrations of these greenhouse gases rise, the average temperature of the lower atmosphere will gradually increase.

Heat Waves - A prolonged period of excessive heat, often combined with excessive humidity.

Hydrocarbons - Substances containing only hydrogen and carbon. Fossil fuels are made up of hydrocarbons.

Hydrologic Cycle - The process of evaporation, vertical and horizontal transport of vapor, condensation, precipitation, and the flow of water from continents to oceans. It is a major factor in determining climate through its influence on surface vegetation, the clouds, snow and ice, and soil moisture. The hydrologic cycle is responsible for 25 to 30 percent of the mid-latitudes' heat transport from the equatorial to polar regions.

Hydrosphere - The component of the climate system comprising liquid surface and subterranean water, such as: oceans, seas, rivers, fresh water lakes, underground water etc.

Industrial Revolution - A period of rapid industrial growth with far-reaching social and economic consequences, beginning in England during the second half of the 18th century and spreading to Europe and later to other countries including the United States. The industrial revolution marks the beginning of a strong increase in combustion of fossil fuels and related emissions of carbon dioxide.

Infrared Radiation - Infrared radiation consists of light whose wavelength is longer than the red color in the visible part of the spectrum, but shorter than microwave radiation. Infrared radiation can be perceived as heat. The Earth's surface, the atmosphere, and clouds all emit infrared radiation, which is also known as terrestrial or long-wave radiation. In contrast, solar radiation is mainly short-wave radiation because of the temperature of the Sun.

Inundation - The submergence of land by water, particularly in a coastal setting.

Landfill - Land waste disposal site in which waste is generally spread in thin layers, compacted, and covered with a fresh layer of soil each day.

Latitude - The location north or south in reference to the equator, which is designated at zero (0) degrees. Lines of latitude are parallel to the equator and circle the globe. The North and South poles are at 90 degrees North and South latitude.

Least Developed Country - A country with low indicators of socioeconomic development and human resources, as well as economic vulnerability, as determined by the United Nations.

Megacities - Cities with populations over 10 million.

Methane (CH_4) - A hydrocarbon that is a greenhouse gas with a global warming potential most recently estimated at 25 times that of carbon dioxide (CO_2). Methane is produced through anaerobic (without oxygen) decomposition of waste in landfills, animal digestion, decomposition of animal wastes, production and distribution of natural gas and petroleum, coal production, and incomplete fossil fuel combustion. The GWP is from the IPCC's Fourth Assessment Report (AR4).

Mitigation - A human intervention to reduce the human impact on the climate system; it includes strategies to reduce greenhouse gas sources and emissions and enhancing greenhouse gas sinks.

Mount Pinatubo - A volcano in the Philippine Islands that erupted in 1991. The eruption of Mount Pinatubo ejected enough particulate and sulfate aerosol matter into the atmosphere to block some of the incoming solar radiation from reaching Earth's atmosphere. This effectively cooled the planet from 1992 to 1994, masking the warming that had been occurring for most of the 1980s and 1990s.

Municipal Solid Waste (MSW) - Residential solid waste and some non-hazardous commercial, institutional, and industrial wastes. This material is generally sent to municipal landfills for disposal.

Natural Gas - Underground deposits of gases consisting of 50 to 90 percent methane (CH_4) and small amounts of heavier gaseous hydrocarbon compounds such as propane (C3H8) and butane (C4H10).

Nitrogen Cycle - The natural circulation of nitrogen among the atmosphere, plants, animals, and microorganisms that live in soil and water. Nitrogen takes on a variety of chemical forms throughout the nitrogen cycle, including nitrous oxide (N_2O) and nitrogen oxides (NOx).

Ocean Acidification - Increased concentrations of carbon dioxide in sea water causing a measurable increase in acidity (i.e., a reduction in ocean pH). This may lead to reduced calcification rates of calcifying organisms such as corals, mollusks, algae and crustaceans.

Oxidize - To chemically transform a substance by combining it with oxygen.

Ozone - Ozone, the triatomic form of oxygen (O_3), is a gaseous atmospheric constituent. In the troposphere, it is created by photochemical reactions involving gases resulting both from natural sources and from human activities (photochemical smog). In high concentrations, tropospheric ozone can be harmful to a wide range of living organisms. Tropospheric ozone acts as a greenhouse gas. In the stratosphere, ozone is created by the interaction between solar ultraviolet radiation and molecular oxygen (O2). Stratospheric ozone plays a decisive role in the stratospheric radiative balance. Depletion of stratospheric ozone, due to chemical reactions that may be enhanced by climate change, results in an increased ground-level flux of ultraviolet (UV-) B radiation.

Ozone Layer - The layer of ozone that begins approximately 15 km above Earth and thins to an almost negligible amount at about 50 km, shields the Earth from harmful ultraviolet radiation from the sun. The highest natural concentration of ozone (approximately 10 parts per million by volume) occurs in the stratosphere at approximately 25 km above Earth. The stratospheric ozone concentration changes throughout the year as stratospheric circulation changes with the seasons. Natural events such as volcanoes and solar flares can produce changes in ozone concentration, but man-made changes are of the greatest concern.

Phenology - The timing of natural events, such as flower blooms and animal migration, which is influenced by changes in climate. Phenology is the study of such important seasonal events. Phenological events are influenced by a combination of climate factors, including light, temperature, rainfall, and humidity.

Photosynthesis - The process by which plants take CO_2 from the air (or bicarbonate in water) to build carbohydrates, releasing O2 in the process. There are several pathways of photosynthesis with different responses to atmospheric CO_2 concentrations.

Recycling - Collecting and reprocessing a resource so it can be used again. An example is collecting aluminum cans, melting them down, and using the aluminum to make new cans or other aluminum products.

Reforestation - Planting of forests on lands that have previously contained forests but that have been converted to some other use.

Relative Sea Level Rise - The increase in ocean water levels at a specific location, taking into account both global sea level rise and local factors, such as local subsidence and uplift. Relative sea level rise is measured with respect to a specified vertical datum relative to the land, which may also be changing elevation over time.

Renewable Energy - Energy resources that are naturally replenishing such as biomass, hydro, geothermal, solar, wind, ocean thermal, wave action, and tidal action.

Resilience - A capability to anticipate, prepare for, respond to, and recover from significant multi-hazard threats with minimum damage to social well-being, the economy, and the environment.

Respiration - The process whereby living organisms convert organic matter to CO_2, releasing energy and consuming O2.

Salt Water Intrusion - Displacement of fresh or ground water by the advance of salt water due to its greater density, usually in coastal and estuarine areas.

Scenarios - A plausible and often simplified description of how the future may develop based on a coherent and internally consistent set of assumptions about driving forces and key relationships.

Sea Surface Temperature - The temperature in the top several feet of the ocean, measured by ships, buoys and drifters.

Sensitivity - The degree to which a system is affected, either adversely or beneficially, by climate variability or change. The effect may be direct (e.g., a change in crop yield in response to a change in the mean, range or variability of temperature) or indirect (e.g., damages caused by an increase in the frequency of coastal flooding due to sea level rise).

Snowpack - A seasonal accumulation of slow-melting snow.

Soil Carbon - A major component of the terrestrial biosphere pool in the carbon cycle. The amount of carbon in the soil is a function of the historical vegetative cover and productivity, which in turn is dependent in part upon climatic variables.

Storm Surge - An abnormal rise in sea level accompanying a hurricane or other intense storm, whose height is the difference between the observed level of the sea surface and the level that would have occurred in the absence of the cyclone.

Stratosphere - Region of the atmosphere between the troposphere and mesosphere, having a lower boundary of approximately 8 km at the poles to 15 km at the equator and an upper boundary of approximately 50 km. Depending upon latitude and season, the temperature in the lower stratosphere can increase, be isothermal, or even decrease with altitude, but the temperature in the upper stratosphere generally increases with height due to absorption of solar radiation by ozone.

Thermal Expansion - The increase in volume (and decrease in density) that results from warming water. A warming of the ocean leads to an expansion of the ocean volume, which leads to an increase in sea level.

Tundra - A treeless, level, or gently undulating plain characteristic of the Arctic and sub-Arctic regions characterized by low temperatures and short growing seasons.

Tsunami - A large wave on the ocean, usually caused by an undersea earthquake, a volcanic eruption, or coastal landslide. A *tsunami* can travel hundreds of miles over the open sea and cause extensive damage when it encounters land. Also called tidal waves.

Ultraviolet Radiation (UV) - The energy range just beyond the violet end of the visible spectrum. Although ultraviolet radiation constitutes only about 5 percent of the total energy emitted from the sun, it is the major energy source for the stratosphere and mesosphere, playing a dominant role in both energy balance and chemical composition. Most ultraviolet radiation is blocked by Earth's atmosphere, but some solar ultraviolet penetrates and aids in plant photosynthesis and helps produce vitamin D in humans. Too much ultraviolet radiation can burn the skin, cause skin cancer and cataracts, and damage vegetation.

United Nations Framework Convention on Climate Change (UNFCCC) - The Convention on Climate Change sets an overall framework for intergovernmental efforts to tackle the challenge posed by climate change. It recognizes that the climate system is a shared resource whose stability can be affected by industrial and other emissions of carbon dioxide and other greenhouse gases. The Convention enjoys near universal membership, with 189 countries having ratified.

Under the Convention, governments:

- gather and share information on greenhouse gas emissions, national policies and best practices

- launch national strategies for addressing greenhouse gas emissions and adapting to expected impacts, including the provision of financial and technological support to developing countries

- cooperate in preparing for adaptation to the impacts of climate change

The Convention entered into force on 21 March 1994.

Vulnerability - The degree to which a system is susceptible to, or unable to cope with, adverse effects of climate change, including climate variability and extremes. Vulnerability is a function of the character, magnitude, and rate of climate variation to which a system is exposed; its sensitivity; and its adaptive capacity.

Wastewater - Water that has been used and contains dissolved or suspended waste materials.

Water Vapor - The most abundant greenhouse gas, it is the water present in the atmosphere in gaseous form. Water vapor is an important part of the natural greenhouse effect. While humans are not significantly increasing its concentration through direct emissions, it contributes to the enhanced greenhouse effect because the warming influence of greenhouse gases leads to a positive water vapor feedback. In addition to its role as a natural greenhouse gas, water vapor also affects the temperature of the planet because clouds form when excess water vapor in the atmosphere condenses to form ice and water droplets and precipitation.

Weather - Atmospheric condition at any given time or place. It is measured in terms of such things as wind, temperature, humidity, atmospheric pressure, cloudiness, and precipitation. In most places, weather can change from hour-to-hour, day-to-day, and season-to-season. Climate in a narrow sense is usually defined as the "average weather", or more rigorously, as the statistical description in terms of the mean and variability of relevant quantities over a period of time ranging from months to thousands or millions of years. The classical period is 30 years, as defined by the World Meteorological Organization (WMO). These quantities are most often surface variables such as temperature, precipitation, and wind. Climate in a wider sense is the state, including a statistical description, of the climate system. A simple way of remembering the difference is that climate is what you expect (e.g. cold winters) and 'weather' is what you get (e.g. a blizzard).

PUZZLES PUZLES

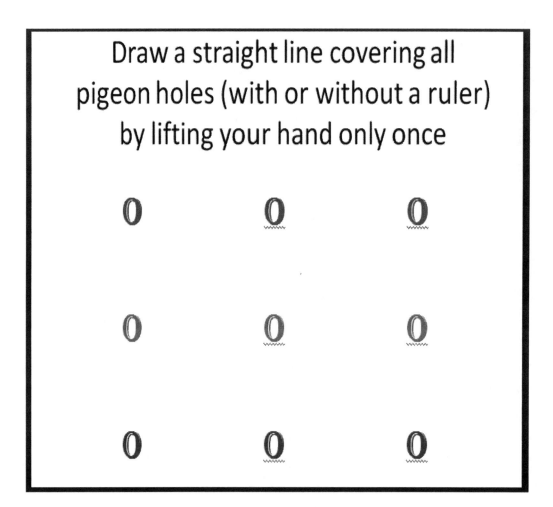

Puzzle 1 – a workshop on creativity

Solutions are in page 370

1. Find the area of the overall skating rink
2. Find the area of the light shaded portion

Red length = 4 meters   Orange radius = 4 meters

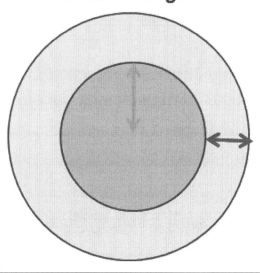

Puzzle 2 – a typical math problem encountered on frequent bases.

Solutions are in page 370

She bought 10 books at a book sale, paid $2 each

for some and $3 each for the rest of the books.

How many books did Febe buy if she spent $26?

Puzzle 3 – a math problem that makes you deeply

ponder when caught off guard.

Solutions are in page 370

HOUSE FOR A HOME

A retired family decide that their new house must have an area of 2,000 square feet. F9 as real estate firm thinks, found the perfect house, but doesn't know the exact area. She tells the family that the house is shape like a rectangle with its length being twice its width. Its perimeter is 240 feet. Is the house big enough for the retired family?

What is the area of the house in meter unit?

Puzzle 4 – alert real estate agency reaction

Solutions are in page 370

FINALS EXAM

A math teacher, was disappointed to announce that only 22% of her 68 students passed the exam. How many students failed the test?

After reviewing the material, the math teacher tested the class again. Now, on the 68 students retested, 75% passed and 12% of those made A's.

How many of her students made an A on the exam?

Puzzle 5 – Finals Exam is simply an exercise to test

our passion for the real estate profession

Solutions are in page 370

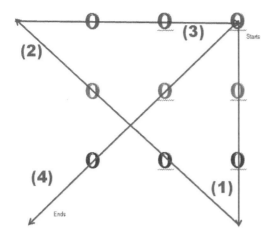

Above is answer to Puzzle 1

1) $A = phi\ r^2 = 3.1416 \times 64 = 200.96\ cm^2$

Then the final area of the small circle

2) $A = phi\ r^2 = 3.1416 \times 16 \quad = 50.24\ cm^2$

Then subtract the area of the small circle

From the area of the big circle to find the

Area of the light shaded circle

$200.96 - 50.24 = 150.72\ cm^2$

Answer to Puzzle 2

Write an algebraic equation. Let n equal the number of $2 books

2n + 3(10-n) = 26

2n + 30-3n = 26 -n = - 4

n = 4 of $2 each

n = 6 of &3 each

Check: 26-8 = 18/3 = 6

Answer to Puzzle 3 = 10 books

Yes. 3,200 square feet

Use the perimeter (240) to determine the of the house

80 feet and the width 40 feet

Area = length x width

3,200 / 10.7584 = 297.44 square meter

Answer to Puzzle 4

1) First, determine the percent failing (78%),

Then multiply by the number of students (68) the answer is 53

2) 68 x 75% = 51 passed; 51 x 12% = 6.12 or 6 Answer to Puzzle 5

MEASUREMENT CONVERSIONS

1 meter is equal to 3.281 feet

$1 \text{ m} = (1/0.3048) \text{ ft} = 3.281\text{ft}$

1 centimeter is equal to 0.394 inches

$1\text{cm} = (1/2.54)'' = 0.394''$

1 centimeter is equal to 10 millimeters

$1 \text{ cm} = 10 \text{ mm}$

1 foot is equal to 30.48 centimeters

$1 \text{ ft} = 30.48 \text{ cm}$

1 foot is equal to 12 inches

$1 \text{ ft} = 12''$

1 foot is equal to 0.305 meters

$1 \text{ ft} = 0.305 \text{ m}$

1 inch is equal to 0.0254 meters

$1'' = 0.0254\text{m}$

1 inch is equal to 1/12 feet

$1'' = 1/12\text{ft} = 0.083\text{ft}$

1 inch is equal to 0.0254 meters

$1'' = 0.0254\text{m}$

1 inch is equal to 25.4 millimeters

$1'' = 25.4\text{mm}$

1 kilometer is equal to 0.6214 miles

$1/1.609) \text{ mi} = 0.621 \text{ mi}$

1 meter is equal to 0.3.281 feet

$1/0.3048) \text{ ft} = 3.281 \text{ ft}$

1 Hectare	=	2.47105381 Acres
1 Hectare	=	107,639,104 Square Feet
1 Hectare	=	15,500,031 Square Meters
1 Hectare	=	10,000 Square Meters
1 Hectare	=	0.00386102159 Square Mile

KILOMETERS TO MILES

Kilometers	Miles	Kilometers	Miles	Kilometers	Miles
1 km	0.62 mi	21 km	13.05 mi	41 km	25.48 mi
2 km	1.24 mi	22 km	13.67 mi	42 km	26.10 mi
3 km	1.86 mi	23 km	14.29 mi	43km	26.72 mi
4 km	2.49 mi	24 km	14.91 mi	44 km	27.34 mi
5 km	3.11 mi	25 km	15.53 mi	45 km	27.96 mi

MILES TO KILOMETERS

Miles	Kilometers	Miles	Kilometers	Miles	Kilometers
1 mi	1.61 km	21 mi	33.80 km	41 mi	65.98 km
2 mi	3.22 km	22 mi	35.41 km	42 mi	67.59 km
3 mi	4.83 km	23 mi	37.01 km	43 mi	69.20 km
4 mi	6.44 km	24 mi	38.62 km	44 mi	70.81 km
5 mi	8.05 km	25 km	40.23 km	45 mi	72.42 km

METERS TO FEET

Meters	Feet	Meters	Feet	Meter	Feet
1 m	3.28 ft	21 m	68.90 ft	41 m	134.51 ft
2 m	6.56 ft	22 m	72.18 ft	42 m	137.80 ft
3 m	9.84 ft	23 m	75.46 ft	43 m	141.08 ft
4 m	13.12 ft	24 m	78.74 ft	44 m	144.36 ft
5 m	16.40 ft	25 m	82.02 ft	45 m	147.64 ft

FEET TO METERS

Feet	Meters	Feet	Meters	Feet	Meters
1 ft	.30 m	21 ft	6.40 m	41 ft	12.50 m
2 ft	.61 m	22 ft	6.71 m	42 ft	12.80 m
3 ft	.91 m	23 ft	7.01 m	43 ft	13.11 m
4 ft	1.22 m	24 ft	7.32 m	44 ft	13.41m
5 ft	1.52 m	25 ft	7.62 m	45 ft	13.72 m

POUNDS TO KILOGRAMS

Pounds	Kilomgrams	Pounds	Kilograms	Pounds	Kilograms
1 lb	.45 kg	21 lb	9.53 kg	41 lb	18.60 kg
2 lb	.91 kg	22 lb	9.98 kg	42 lb	19.05 kg
3 lb	1.36 kg	23 lb	10.43 kg	43 lb	19.50 kg
4 lb	1.81 kg	24 ft	10.89 kg	44 ft	19.96 kg
5 lb	2.27 kg	25 ft	11.34 kg	45 ft	20.41 kg

KILOGRAMS TO POUNDS

Kilograms	Pounds	Kilograms	Pounds	Kilograms	Pounds
1 kg	2.2 lb	21 kg	46.30 lb	41 kg	90.39 lb
2 kg	4.41 lb	22 kg	48.50 lb	42 kg	92.59 lb
3 kg	6.61 lb	23 kg	50. 71 lb	43 kg	94.80 lb
4 kg	8.82 lb	24 kg	52.91 lb	44 kg	97.00 lb
5 kg	11.02 lb	25 kg	55.12 lb	45 kg	99.21 lb

FAHRENHEIT TO CELSIUS

Conversion from Fahrenheit **to** Celsius **Formula**

$$C = (°F - 32) / 1.8$$

Fahrenheit	Celsius	Fahrenheit	Celsius	Fahrenheit	Celsius
1 F	-17.22C	21 F	-6.11 C	41 F	5.00 C
2 F	-16.67 C	22 F	-5.56 C	42 F	5.56 C
3 F	-16.11 C	23 F	-5.00 C	43 F	6.11 C
4 F	-15.56 C	24 F	-4.44 C	44 F	6.67 C
5 F	-15.00 C	25 F	-3.89 C	45 F	7.22 C

CELSIUS TO FAHRENHEIT

Conversion from Celsius **to** Fahrenheit **Formula**

$$F = °C \times 1.8 + 32$$

Celsius	Fahrenheit	Celsius	Fahrenheit	Celsius	Fahrenheit
1 C	33.80 F	21 C	69.80F	41 C	105.80 F
2 C	35.60 F	22 C	71.60 F	42 C	107.60 F
3 C	37.40 F	23 C	73.40 F	43 C	109.40 F
4 C	39.20 F	24 C	75.20 F	44 C	111.20 F
5 C	41.00 F	25 C	77.00 F	45 C	113.00 F

Period	1%	5.00%	10.00%	15.00%	20.00%	25.00%
1.00	$1.0100	$1.0500	$1.1000	$1.1500	$1.2000	$1.2500
2.00	$1.0201	$1.1025	$1.2100	$1.3225	$1.4400	$1.5625
3.00	$1.0303	$1.1576	$1.3310	$1.5209	$1.7280	$1.9531
4.00	$1.0406	$1.2155	$1.4641	$1.7490	$2.0736	$2.4414
5.00	$1.0510	$1.2763	$1.6105	$2.0114	$2.4883	$2.4414
6.00	$1.0615	$1.3401	$1.7716	$2.3131	$2.9860	$3.8147
7.00	$1.0721	$1.4071	$1.9487	$2.6600	$3.5832	$4.7684
8.00	$1.0829	$1.4775	$2.1436	$3.0590	$4.2998	$5.9605
9.00	$1.0937	$1.5513	$2.3579	$3.5159	$5.1598	$7.4506
10.00	$1.1046	$1.6289	$2.5937	$4.0456	$6.1917	$9.3132
11.00	$1.1157	$1.7303	$2.8531	$4.6524	$7.4301	$11.6415
12.00	$1.1268	$1.7959	$3.1384	$5.3503	$8.9161	$14.5519
13.00	$1.1381	$1.8856	$3.4523	$6.1528	$10.6993	$18.1899
14.00	$1.1495	$1.9799	$3.7975	$7.0757	$12.8392	$22.7374
15.00	$1.1610	$2.0789	$4.1772	$8.1371	$15.4070	$28.4217
16.00	$1.1726	$2.1829	$4.5950	$9.3576	$18.4884	$35.5271
17.00	$1.1843	$2.2920	$5.0545	$10.7613	$22.1861	$44.4089

18.00	$1.1961	$2.4066	$5.5599	$12.3755	$26.6233	$55.5112
19.00	$1.2081	$2.5270	$6.1159	$14.2318	$31.9480	$69.3889
20.00	$1.2202	$2.6533	$6.7275	$16.3665	$38.3376	$86.7362

FUTURE VALUE OF $1 INVESTED TODAY

AT THE END OF N PERIOD

$$FV = PV (1 + i)^N$$

PRESENT VALUE OF OF $1

PER PERIOD FOR N PERIODS (PVIF)

$$PV = FV (1 + i)^N$$

Period	1%	5.00%	10.00%	15.00%	20.00%	25.00%	30.00%
1.00	$0.9901	$0.9524	$0.9091	$0.8696	$0.8333	$0.8000	$0.7692
2.00	$0.9803	$0.9070	$0.8264	$0.7561	$0.6944	$0.6400	$0.5917
3.00	$0.9706	$0.8638	$0.7513	$0.6575	$0.5787	$0.5120	$0.4552
4.00	$0.9610	$0.8227	$0.6830	$0.5718	$0.4823	$0.4096	$0.3501
5.00	$0.9515	$0.7835	$0.6209	$0.4972	$0.4019	$0.3277	$0.2693
6.00	$0.9420	$0.7462	$0.5645	$0.4323	$0.3349	$0.2621	$0.2072
7.00	$0.9327	$0.7107	$0.5132	$0.3759	$0.2791	$0.2097	$0.1594
8.00	$0.9235	$0.6768	$0.4665	$0.3269	$0.2326	$0.1678	$0.1226
9.00	$0.9143	$0.6446	$0.4241	$0.2843	$0.1938	$0.1342	$0.0943
10.00	$0.9053	$0.6139	$0.3855	$0.2472	$0.1615	$0.1074	$0.0725

11.00	$0.8963	$0.5847	$0.3505	$0.2149	$0.1346	$0.0859	$0.0558
12.00	$0.8874	$0.5568	$0.3186	$0.1869	$0.1122	$0.0687	$0.0429
13.00	$0.8787	$0.5303	$0.2897	$0.1625	$0.0935	$0.0550	$0.0330
14.00	$0.8700	$0.5051	$0.2633	$0.1413	$0.0779	$0.0440	$0.0254
15.00	$0.8613	$0.4810	$0.2394	$0.1229	$0.0649	$0.0352	$0.0195
16.00	$0.8528	$0.4581	$0.2176	$0.1069	$0.0541	$0.0281	$0.0150
17.00	$0.8444	$0.4363	$0.1978	$0.0929	$0.0451	$0.0225	$0.0116
18.00	$0.8360	$0.4155	$0.1799	$0.0808	$0.0376	$0.0180	$0.0089
19.00	$0.8277	$0.3957	$0.1635	$0.0703	$0.0313	$0.0144	$0.0068
20.00	$0.8195	$0.3769	$0.1486	$0.0611	$0.0261	$0.0115	$0.0053

INDEX

subjects/courses 98

supply and demand 201

SWOT 5

T

top notchers 261, 282

U

UAAP 282

V

Value Opinion 227, 233

von Thunen (theorist) 94

W

Wiles, Andrew 41

the wisdom 280

REFERENCE

Engineering Economy by Jaime R. Tiong

January 8, 2002

MBA Management Models by sue Harding and Trevor Long 1996

Business Valuation DeMYSTiFieD by Edward Nelling, Ph.D.

Business Ethics 15th Edition by John E. Richardson

Annual Editions

System for Success by Michael J. Lipsey 2003

Accountingweekly.com/steps-in-the-business-valuation

Business valuation - Wikipedia

https://en.wikipedia.org/wiki/Business_valuation

Dr. Stanley Feldman

Gross Income Multiplier

www.property-investing.org

TVMCalcs.com: Time Value of Money

www.tvmcalcs.com/ by Timothy R. Mayes, Ph.d.

https://en.wikipedia.org/wiki/Muncie,_Indiana

Math Brainteasers by April Bakely

Writing a book is no easy feat. It takes persistence, hard work, and a vast knowledge of the subject at hand. My grandfather possesses all of these qualities. It has been a wonderful experience to be able to witness the progress that he made day-by-day during the writing of his publication. I hope that this book will bring him great success and acknowledgement in the future.

SamSam - spelling bee/tennis champion

It is such a privilege to watch and experience the process of how this book was created by my grandfather. Day by day he spent countless hours putting in his best effort to make this project the best it could possibly be. This experience has taught me that no matter your age, anything is possible with creativity and ambition

SaSha – spelling bee/tennis Champion

Printed in the United States
By Bookmasters